ROASTS AND TOASTS MADE EASY

A Practical Guide for the Creation of Roasts/Toasts for Business and Social Occasions

By

Larry Miller

This book is a work of fiction. Places, events, and situations in this story are purely fictional. Any resemblance to actual persons, living or dead, is coincidental.

ISBN: 1-4033-6578-4 (e-book)
ISBN: 1-4033-6579-2 (Paperback)

Library of Congress Control Number: 2002111736

This book is printed on acid free paper.

Printed in the United States of America
Bloomington, IN

1stBooks - rev. 10/3/02

Table of contents

PREFACE

The initial inspiration for this book was based on numerous occasions when I have been asked to participate in the "Roasting" of a professional or personal friend. The first ones were very difficult exercises. Finally, after awhile, I was able to develop a logical, systematic system capable of producing a suitable and enjoyable Roast, quickly and efficiently. Based on my newly acquired "expertise," friends began to ask me to help them when they either volunteered or were drafted to be a presenter at a Roast.

All of these people were intelligent, accomplished professionals with varying amounts of public speaking experience. Yet, when it came to putting together an appropriate Roast, they were at ground zero, with no idea of what to do nor where to begin.

Therefore, it occurred to me that there is a need for a handbook to assist people in this endeavor. I then realized that many people also have the need to be able to propose proper Toasts at functions, as well as business meetings and weddings.

Roast and Toast presentations are opportunities to greatly add to the enjoyment of the occasion for which they are used. If done properly, with good humor and taste, they can greatly enhance the reputation of the presenter as well as the enjoyment of the event.

There is a need as well as a potential benefit to use this book as a tool to create a proper presentation in a reasonable amount of time when called upon to Roast or Toast someone.

In it you will find a full-blown description of how to create an appropriate Roast with actual Roast and joke samples to assist you in creating your own.

The Toast section is mainly a listing of occasions such as weddings, retirement parties, and appropriate Toasts.

This book should be a standard item in the library of anyone who can be called upon to deliver Roasts and/or Toasts in their business or personal lives and is also a wonderful gift for such a person.

ACKNOWLEDGMENTS

I would like to thank all my friends who continually encouraged me to do this project. I am especially indebted to Bob Cowan for his help in organizing and researching much of the source material for this book.

And last, but not least, my wife Carole is owed a large debt of gratitude for her help in reviewing and entering much of the material, and giving me the incentive to move ahead.

INTRODUCTION

Most people are uncomfortable when asked to speak in front of family members, close friends, acquaintances and complete strangers. This book will show how to make the presentation easier than in the past when you are expected to address a group of people. When done properly, you should be admired and appreciated by your audience.

Two kinds of presentations which you may be called upon to deliver are Roasts and Toasts. This book covers these subjects in that order. Always remember that the goal is to add to the enjoyment of an already happy occasion.

Very few of us are born presenters. You may be shy and lack a sense of humor, but if you follow the guide we have prepared, you will be able to do a credible job of preparing and presenting a Roast or a Toast. The transformation is not magic. Don't you remember the person you knew in high school as a clumsy and shy individual who turned out to be a top litigator? What changed? An appropriate education and early in his/her law career, one had no choice and had to stand before a judge and jury and become eloquent or find another "day job."

The three keys to a successful Roast or Toast are: preparation, preparation, and more preparation. We all are aware of the writing staff that supports the successful (and sometimes unsuccessful) Hollywood comedians. On the nights the comedian is "off", it is the fault of the material, and when the comedian has a wonderful night, it is his/her own doing, and the writers are forgotten.

An old time Catskill ventriloquist was starving and goes to his business manager to complain. His manager tells him, "Ventriloquists are out. Everything is 'New Age', 'dot.com' and related subjects. If you want to work ever again, you must change your focus." The ventriloquist was shaken but vowed to himself that he could make the change. He went to the local bookstore (he didn't have the Net available) and bought a selection of books from the "New Age" section and read them from cover to cover in a few weeks. Before the month was over, he had a sign posted on his front door that notified the neighborhood that a Channeler was available. Before he could finish his breakfast after posting his sign, his doorbell rang, and his first potential client entered his living room. She asked him a few perfunctory questions and then asked about the price: "If I talk to your deceased husband, $25.00, if you talk to your deceased husband, the fee will be $50.00, and if you talk to your deceased husband while I'm drinking a glass of water, $100.00."

The morphing from ventriloquist to Channeler, required some preparation, but it made a new career from one that was failing. A good stage presence can be learned, and it will be necessary to be comfortable standing in front of others and sharing the spotlight with the target (Roastee). However, the microphone, if one is used, is not shared. The Roaster must rely on his/her learned skills and carry the weight on his/her shoulders.

Above all, when you have been asked to be a presenter of a Roast or a Toast, you should consider it an honor and an opportunity. A well designed and well executed presentation can change the way that you are perceived by those in the audience.

In summary, remember the ABCs and XYZs of public speaking: Always Be Confident and Examine Your Zipper.

WHAT IS A ROAST

A Roast is simply a gathering of people for the purpose of honoring a mutual friend by discussing the honoree in a manner that brings tears of laughter rather than tears of sorrow to the gathering. The key is the material you will be using. The material should be pertinent to the Roastee's situation, be in good taste and capable of being integrated into a presentation.

Good Taste

There are few things more upsetting than sitting through a performance of an artist whose entire repertoire is composed of shock value material. A good Roast does not require profanity nor material in poor taste. When the attendees refrain from laughing and avert the eyes of others, the Roast has crossed over the line, and the Roaster needs to redeem himself. The best Roast will have both the audience and the Roastee laughing at, but not embarrassed by, your presentation.

Your goal is not to reveal any hurtful skeletons in the closet that you know about the Roastee. Such secrets are best left in the closet and are not worth the pain they may bring to the Roastee or other attendees. The events that occurred 35 years ago after a high school football game may bring a smile to your face but may be unpleasant for the Roastee to recall.

Capable of Being Integrated

The raw material you have to work with is your knowledge of the Roastee, stories about the Roastee you are able to glean from friends, and your ability to tailor some of the raw material herein provided into the presentation and thereby personalizing it to meet your needs. It is a sure bet that the raw material you can glean from a variety of sources can be adapted to the Roastee with just little, if any, change. As you will see in the examples, the material presented can be based on factual events or can be totally made up to make a point and/or get a laugh.

Always remember that you are there to entertain, so anything that is in good taste and gets a laugh is appropriate, whether or not it is true.

TYPES OF ROASTS

Roasts can be considered formal and informal. The term formal denotes the nature of the event. If it is a business or social occasion where the audience is well dressed, it suggests the formal Roast. On the other hand, a gathering of friends and acquaintances suggests an informal Roast.

The Formal Roast

Clearly some circumstances dictate a sense of formality. A 50th birthday party held at the local 5-star hotel will require the Roaster(s) to be appropriately dressed, and your material should be well prepared and suitable for the tone of the event.

The Roaster should plan on working from a speaker's podium, and, if there are co-Roasters, they could be seated at a draped speakers' table. You will need to check that microphones are available and are placed where the Roaster(s) will be seated. Suitable sites for a formal Roast will likely have a logistics person available to advise you regarding the room preparation. If you intend to use audio visual technology, you can use your own or rent it. First class hotels and banquet halls often maintain a stock of such equipment and can provide it inexpensively. If they do not have equipment available, they know where it can be rented. If you are able to find some, old home videos, movies, or pictures of the Roastee are an ideal mood setter and can provide some basic material for you to use in your Roast.

Informal Roast

These take the form of anything ranging from a gathering of a group of friends at your home to an interlude during a business meeting. Depending on the size of the group, a microphone may be needed. Use a written script or cue cards if they will help your delivery, but don't forget to look up at the Roastee and the audience at appropriate times.

PREPARATION FOR THE ROAST

One very convenient aspect to preparing a Roast is that the material you need already exists in hundreds of books of jokes and biographies of comedians and writers. Don't be fooled into thinking that all material you deliver must be original. With the existence of the Internet and worldwide instantaneous communication, many people spend much of their non-working hours writing and exchanging jokes with others who have similar interests. Your material can be as up-to-the-minute as today's news.

In this manual you will likely find much of the Roasting material needed. However, it is necessary to modify the material to personalize it to fit the occasion. For example: "My daughter is happily married. Her husband is scared to death of her" can be changed to "The Roastee's wife is happily married. He is scared to death of her" or "The Roastee is such a tough landlord that when one of his tenants complained of roaches, the Roastee raised the rent because the tenant was keeping pets." These are just two examples of modifying one liner's to fit a specific Roast situation. One additional caveat applies. Unless you are a native speaker of language other than English, don't try to present your material with an accent. You may offend or embarrass people in the audience.

In order to create an appropriate Roast, it is important to first know something about the Roastee. The following questionnaire will help you document most of the data you will need. If you are a close, long-time acquaintance of the Roastee, you probably know most, if not all, of this information. If not, you can find out what you need to know by asking around. It is not imperative to have all the data on the form, but whatever you do have will be helpful.

After filling out the form, it is important to have some reference books available. One type of book is a collection of jokes that are grouped by topic and referenced in an index. Many such books are available in bookstores. Similar reference material can easily be found using any of the popular search engines on the Internet.

A second reference book is a book of poems that may have an appropriate thought for either the introduction or closing of the Roast. You can also find these in bookstores or in the public library, if you do not already own one.

If you can get by with the jokes and poems in this book, you will not need anything else.

ROASTEE QUESTIONNAIRE

1. Name

2. Is this Roast for a specific event?

    * Birthday

    * Anniversary

    * Retirement

    * Promotion

    * Etc.

3. About the Roastee

4. A) Marriage status

    * How many?

    * How long?

    * Wife's(s') name(s)?

   B) Education

    * Schools

    * Degrees

    * Honors

   C) Jobs

    * What?

    * How long?

    * Where?

   D) Quirks

    * Behavior

    * Appearance/mannerisms

    * Dress

7

    E) Hobbies and interests

        *   Sports

        *   Cultural

        *   Collections

        *   Vacations

    F) Family

        *   Children (and grandchildren)

        *   Names, number, and ages

        *   Close relatives

    G) Specific incidents to reference

        *   Something (usually humorous) which involved the Roastee

    H) Your relationship to Roastee

ACTUAL ROAST SAMPLES

The following Roasts were prepared using the guidelines in this book. The results were outstanding. Everyone, including the Roastees, enjoyed them, and the Roasts added a lot to an already enjoyable evening.

As you can see from these examples, the Roast consists of three main parts as follows:

1. The Introduction - This serves as the lead-in to the main body of the Roast.
2. The Main Body - This is where most of the Roast material is found.
3. The Conclusion - This ends the Roast on a high note.

SAMPLE ROAST #1

ROASTEE QUESTIONNAIRE

1. Name: Dan Smith

2. Is this Roast for a specific event?
    *   Birthday
    *   Anniversary
    *   Retirement
    *   Promotion
    *   Etc. — Graduation - Ph.D. - Psychology

3. About the Roastee

4. A) Marriage status: Single
    *   How many?
    *   How long?
    *   Wife's (s') name(s)?
    B) Education
    *   Schools
    *   Degrees - Ph.D.
    *   Honors
    C) Jobs
    *   What? - Various sales jobs
    *   How long?

     *   Where?

D) Quirks

     *   Behavior

     *   Appearance/mannerisms

     *   Dress

E) Hobbies and interests

     *   Sports

     *   Cultural — Music

     *   Collections

     *   Vacations

F) Family

     *   Children (and grandchildren)

     *   Names, number, and ages

     *   Close relatives — Mom, dad, 2 brothers

G) Specific incidents to reference

     *   Something (usually humorous) which involved the Roastee — Took a long time to graduate

H) Your relationship to Roastee — Long time friend, neighbor, and school mate

SAMPLE ROAST #1

This Roast was written for someone who was asked to be a Roaster at his friend's graduation party. It was a very happy event and everyone agreed that the Roast was one of the highlights of the evening. There were about 70 people present and they all laughed during the Roast and applauded after it was over.

ROAST FOR DAN SMITH FOR HIS PH.D. GRADUATION

Good evening. My name is Bill Roberts. Tonight we are gathered to pay tribute to a man who deserves the accolades of every person here - a man with incredible charm and intelligence, a man who has worked hard and accomplished much and is an outstanding example for all who know him. But enough about me, let's get on with the Roast.

I am very happy to be here to honor my good friend, Dan Smith. I've known Dan for over twenty years, so I feel qualified to give some insights into who he really is and share with you some things about him that you may not have known.

Even as a young boy, Dan demonstrated analytical abilities which allowed him to discern fact from fiction, a quality which would serve him well in the field of psychology. One Sunday, Dan came home from religious school and told his father that he had heard a fantastic story. The Jews were chased out of Egypt, and they came to the Red Sea. When they saw the Egyptians following them, they built a bridge over the Red Sea and crossed over in safety. When the Egyptians kept coming, the Jews put dynamite under the bridge and when all the Egyptians were on the bridge, the Jews blew it up, and the Egyptians fell into the sea and drowned. His Dad asked, "Did your teacher really tell you this story?" "No," answered Dan, "but if I told you what she told us, you'd never believe it."

Psychologists often want to know about a patient's relationship with his/her family members. Dan has a good relationship with his mother, and he always wanted to be helpful around the house. One Mother's Day, the whole family got together for a big dinner with friends. Afterward, when Mom started to clean up, Dan said, "Don't worry about the dishes Mom. Today is Mother's Day. You can always do them tomorrow."

Once, his Mom bought Dan two new ties. He ran to his room and immediately put one on and returned, beaming, to his mother's room. He said, "Look Mom. Isn't it gorgeous?" She said, "What's the matter? You don't like the other one?"

When Dan was young, his Mom often made chocolate cake with frosting from scratch. She would even let Dan lick the beaters, and she'd turn them off when he was through.

Dan has two brothers, Jeff and Mike, and the three of them were quite mischievous as little kids. Whenever something went wrong in the neighborhood, it nearly always turned out they had a hand in it. His parents didn't know what to do, so they approached their pastor and asked for advice. The pastor said he would talk to the boys, but he wanted to talk to Dan alone first because he was the oldest. He sat Dan across from the huge desk he sat behind, and they stared at each other in silence for five minutes. Finally, the pastor pointed a finger at Dan and asked, "Where is G-d?" Dan looked under the desk and around the room, but said nothing. Again, louder, the pastor pointed at Dan and asked, "Where is G-d?" Again, Dan looked around the room and said nothing. A third time, in a louder, firmer voice, the pastor leaned far over the desk, put his finger almost to Dan's nose and asked, "Where is G-d?" Dan panicked and ran all the way home. He found Mike and Jeff and dragged them into the fort where they usually plotted their mischief and said, "We're in big trouble." Jeff asked, "What do you mean?" Dan said, "G-d is missing, and they think we did it!"

Dan has managed to remain a bachelor so far, and he likes to consider himself a ladies' man, but what you may not realize is he focuses on homeless women because he knows it's easier to talk them into spending the night.

Dan has a prolific dating history. In fact, he's been on so many blind dates, he qualifies for a free dog.

I remember a conversation that I had with Dan early in our college years. We were discussing our futures and career plans. I told Dan that I wanted to go to dental school and specialize in oral surgery. He said, "Are you crazy? That could take you ten years. There's no way I'd ever stay in school that long." Dan, congratulations on your fifteen years of college.

Well, Dan, you have now paid your dues. Congratulations on your successful completion of your Ph.D. It's now time to start living your life. I want to read a short poem by Edgar Guest about living:

The miser thinks he's living when he's hoarding up his gold;

The soldier calls it living when he's doing something bold.

The sailor thinks it's living to be tossed upon the sea,

And upon this vital subject, no two of us agree.

But I hold to the opinion, as I walk my way along,

That living's made of laughter, good friendship and of song.

SAMPLE ROAST #2

ROASTEE QUESTIONNAIRE

1. Name: Dr. William Brown

2. Is this Roast for a specific event?
    * Birthday — 65th
    * Anniversary
    * Retirement
    * Promotion
    * Etc.

3. About the Roastee

4. A) Marriage status:
    * How many? — One
    * How long? — 30+ years
    * Wife's name? — Joan
   B) Education
    * Schools
    * Degrees — M.D. — Pediatrics
    * Honors
   C) Jobs
    * What?
    * How long?

    *   Where?

D) Quirks

    *   Behavior

    *   Appearance/mannerisms

    *   Dress

E) Hobbies and interests

    *   Sports

    *   Cultural — Music — piano

    *   Collections

    *   Vacations

    *   Miscellaneous — Photography

F) Family

    *   Children (and grandchildren) — 2 children, 4 grandchildren

    *   Names, number, and ages

    *   Close relatives

G) Specific incidents to reference

    *   Something (usually humorous) which involved the Roastee

H) Your relationship to Roastee — Friends and colleagues for many years

SAMPLE ROAST #2

This Roast was written for a good friend of mine who was asked to be a Roaster for a good friend of his. Although my friend had much experience in giving speeches around the world, he was at a standstill in knowing how to create an appropriate Roast. Using the principles in this book, the Roast shown here was put together in less than two hours. The occasion was a dinner with approximately one hundred people present to celebrate a significant birthday of the Roastee.

The Roast was a huge success. The jokes had everyone laughing, and the ending poem brought tears to the Roastee's eyes. My friend is still receiving compliments for his presentation, even though many months have passed.

ROAST FOR DR. WILLIAM BROWN

Good evening. My name is Barry White. I must say, when I was asked to participate in this Roast, I felt like Zsa Zsa Gabor's fifth husband. I had a pretty good idea of what had to be done but was concerned about how to make it interesting. Anyway, even with that concern, I am very happy to be here to honor my good friend and colleague, Bill Brown. I've known Bill for over thirty years, so I feel qualified to give some insights into who Bill really is and share with you some things about Bill that you may not have known.

Of course, I can't talk about Bill without also including Joan, his loving wife of many years. When they were dating, Bill's mother asked him, "Why did you decide to go steady with Joan?" He replied that she was very different from all the other girls he had dated. "How so?" asked his mother. "She's the only one who ever agreed to a second date!" Bill said.

After the first few dates, Bill proposed marriage, saying that he stayed up all night thinking of her. Joan said, "Of course I love you, but why are you proposing to me so soon after we met?" Bill, always the romantic, replied, "I just gotta get some sleep."

Recently, Bill asked Joan, "Will you love me when I'm old and feeble?" and Joan replied, "Of course I do."

Of course, you all know that Bill is a respected physician specializing in pediatrics. He has had many successful cases, but the other day, I asked him what was the biggest mistake he has ever made. He replied that early in his career, he was treating a multi-millionaire's son, and he cured him in only two visits. He learned from this experience, and, shortly afterwards, he had another wealthy patient whom he also successfully treated. The patient was grateful and asked Bill what the cost of his services would be. Bill replied, "$1,000.00 down and $100.00 per month for the next thirty-six months." The astonished patient said, "Boy, that's just like buying a car!" "I just did," replied Bill.

Of course, like all doctors, Bill has had occasional problems with collections. In fact, just recently, one of his patients was asked by his wife whether to pay the electric company or the doctor. The patient immediately replied, "Pay the electric company first because the doctor can't shut off my blood supply."

Being a great diagnostician, Bill recently had a female patient whom he diagnosed with acute indigestion. The patient said, "Now look, doctor, I came here to be examined, not complimented!"

In addition to being a wonderful husband, father, grandfather, and physician, Bill has a great love of the arts, especially music. When he was a young man, he was taking piano lessons. After a while, his mother asked him how it was going. Bill replied that everything was fine and also noted that his teacher was very religious. "How do you know that?" said his mother. "Well, every time I play, the teacher cries out, 'Oh my G-d, my G-d.'"

Then Bill tried to play the violin, but every time he played, tears came to his eyes, so his teacher recommended he stuff cotton in his ears.

Later in life, he was an organist but had to give it up because the monkey died.

Another hobby Bill has is photography. Having a good sense of humor, he recently told me a photography joke. He asked me, "What did the photographer tell Snow White?" I said, "I don't know. What?" "Don't worry, miss, some day your *prints* will come."

I'd like to conclude by dedicating an Edgar Guest poem entitled "A Friend" to my dear friend Bill:

> A friend is one who takes your hand
> And talks a speech you understand.
> He's partly kindness, partly mirth
> And faith unfaltering in your worth.

He's first to cheer you on success

And last to leave you in distress.

A friend is constant, honest, true

In short, old pal, he's just like you.

Happy birthday, dear friend!

SAMPLE ROAST #3

ROASTEE QUESTIONNAIRE

1. Name: Jim White

2. Is this Roast for a specific event?

    * Birthday — 65th

    * Anniversary

    * Retirement

    * Promotion

    * Etc.

3. About the Roastee

4. A) Marriage status:

    * How many?

    * How long? — 10 years

    * Wife's name? — Beverly — 2nd wife

    B) Education

    * Schools

    * Degrees

    * Honors

    C) Jobs

    * What? — Financial Advisor

    * How long?

    * Where?

D) Quirks

* Behavior — Have had many houses — now living in Big Bear (snow country)

    * Appearance/mannerisms — Nervous

    * Dress

E) Hobbies and interests

    * Sports — Hiking

    * Cultural

    * Collections

    * Vacations

F) Family

    * Children (and grandchildren) — Many

    * Names, number, and ages

    * Close relatives

G) Specific incidents to reference

    * Something (usually humorous) which involved the Roastee

H) Your relationship to Roastee — Friend

SAMPLE ROAST #3

This was a Roast I was asked to do for a long time friend. There were about 60 people present and the birthday party took place on a boat cruising the bay. The Roast was greatly enjoyed by all, but as it turns out, there was a major negative factor.

As it turns out, quite a few people had agreed to participate in the Roast. As is typical, all of them had not really prepared much and were planning to tell one or two anecdotes about their experiences with the Roastee.

As it turned out, I was asked to go first and by the time I had finished, most of the other Roasters refused to go on since they felt they would look bad in comparison. Therefore, if you are ever in this type of situation, you might consider asking to go last.

ROAST FOR JIM WHITE FOR HIS 65TH BIRTHDAY

Hi. My name is Bill Mills and my wife, Carole and I have known the Whites' for almost as long as they have known each other.

I'm indeed honored to be speaking this evening. All of you should also feel sincerely honored since at this event, we'll have the opportunity to meet a person who deserves the respect and accolades of everyone here — a person of incredible charm and intelligence — a person of unquestioned integrity, honesty and capability, who has worked hard, accomplished much and is an outstanding example to all. But enough about Bev. Let's get on with a few words about Jim.

A few minutes ago, I spoke to Jim's family, and they implored me to go easy on him. Let me assure you, that no matter how cruel the jokes may appear, no matter how vicious the insults may seem, no matter how embarrassing his exploits may sound, I am respecting their wishes and going easy on Jim.

I want you to remember that regardless of what I am about to say, Jim is a tremendous example to those young people who say, "I don't want an education; I don't want to work hard to achieve a good life; I don't want to be a responsible person." We can point to Jim and say to them, "If you don't change your attitudes, this is how you will turn out!"

Now, before Jim met Bev, he liked to think of himself as the happy man-about-town bachelor. However, even in that mode, Jim had his challenges. During that time, he had so many blind dates, he qualified for a free seeing eye dog. He tried to solve his problem by dating homeless women but still had no luck in getting them to stay the night in his place. But Jim always treated his dates like royalty. He took them to Burger King and Dairy Queen.

But once he met Bev, things changed. In fact, when a friend asked him how come he was seeing her so often, he stated that she was very different from all the other women he had met. "How so?" asked his friend. "She's the only one who ever agreed to a second date," said Jim.

After a while, Jim proposed marriage, saying that he was staying up all night thinking of her. Bev said, "Of course I love you, but why are you proposing to me so soon after we met?" Jim, always the romantic, replied, "I just gotta get some sleep!"

Recently, Jim asked Bev, "Will you still love me when I'm old and feeble?" Bev immediately replied, "Of course I do."

I don't wish to imply that Jim is over the hill, but recently, they sneaked away for a romantic second honeymoon. On the first night, Jim held Bev's hand and promptly fell asleep. The next night, the same thing happened. On the third night, when Jim reached for Bev's hand, she looked at him crossly and said, "Are you some kind of sex maniac? Three nights in a row!"

Before Jim went into business for himself, he had many jobs. His friend asked him why he lost his last job. "A lot of reasons," said Jim. "The shoddy work, the vile language, the sloppiness, the inconsistent work hours — they just wouldn't put up with them anymore."

Of course, you all know that Jim has become quite the expert in financial planning and accounting practices. But even this has its challenges. Jim once received a call from a client who was furious about the charges on his monthly statement. He accused Jim of being a greedy blood-sucker who was taking advantage of his clients. Jim listened intently and finally shouted, "You are such an ingrate to say these things, especially since I just named my yacht after you!"

But since Jim is in the investment business, he meets all kinds of people with their own ideas of the importance of money. One day, a client was opening the door of his BMW when suddenly, a car came along and hit the door, ripping it off completely. When the police came, the man was complaining bitterly about the damage to his precious BMW. "Officer, look what they did to my Beemer," he whined. "You are so materialistic, worrying about your stupid BMW that you didn't even notice that your left arm is ripped off and missing," said the cop. "Oh my G-d," said the client, finally noticing the bloody left shoulder where his arm once was. "Where's my Rolex?"

But Jim is always concerned about his clients. In fact, one day he was walking along the beach when he found a lamp, rubbed it and a genie appeared. The genie agreed to grant Jim one wish in appreciation for his releasing him. Jim said he would like a bridge between California and Hawaii since he didn't like to fly. The genie said that the work to put in the pilings and pour the concrete to build the bridge would be difficult, even for a genie, and he asked Jim to make another wish. "Well," Jim said, "I'm a financial advisor who has many clients. Please make all my clients satisfied with my advice, insure that they have reasonable expectations, and have them never complain if things do not go well with the stock market." The genie paused, sighed, and then asked, "Two lanes or four?"

Well, as you know, Jim and Bev have moved a few times before finally building their dream house in Big Bear. They are very happy there, but I remember when they used to hate the rain when they lived in Orange County. Now they love it when it rains, since they discovered that you don't have to shovel it. But the weather up there is really not so bad. In fact, this winter, it only snowed twice — once for two weeks and once for three weeks.

I'd like to conclude with an Edgar Guest poem entitled "A Friend."

A friend is one who takes your hand

And talks a speech you understand.

He's partly kindness, partly mirth

And faith unfaltering in your worth.

He's first to cheer you on success

And last to leave you in distress.

A friend is constant, honest, true

In short, old pal, he's just like you.

Here's to a happy birthday to my friend, Jim White.

SAMPLE ROAST #4

ROASTEE QUESTIONNAIRE

1. Name: Mike Miller

2. Is this Roast for a specific event?
    *   Birthday — 65th
    *   Anniversary
    *   Retirement
    *   Promotion
    *   Etc.

3. About the Roastee
    A) Marriage status — Married
    *   How many? — One
    *   How long? — 3 years
    *   Wife's name? — Joan
    B) Education
    *   Schools — CCNU, Berkeley
    *   Degrees — BS, MS, Ph.D. - Chemical Engineering
    *   Honors
    C) Jobs
    *   What? — Various
    *   How long?
    *   Where?

D) Quirks

* Behavior

* Appearance/mannerisms

* Dress

E) Hobbies and interests

* Sports — Handball

* Cultural

* Collections

* Vacations

F) Family

* Children (and grandchildren)

* Names, number, and ages

* Close relatives

G) Specific incidents to reference

* Something (usually humorous) which involved the Roastee — Married late in life

H) Your relationship to Roastee — Long time friend

SAMPLE ROAST #4

This is a good example of how a great Roast can be produced quickly on short notice. The Roast was to be presented at a good friend's 65th birthday party. Virtually the entire Roast was put together by cutting and pasting parts from other Roasts. Since the audience for this event was totally different from those at the other Roasts, the repetition was not a problem.

It took less than two hours to write this Roast. It was a huge success with many people literally laughing until it hurt.

My friend really appreciated this entertaining presentation which was the highlight of the evening.

At least 10 people came up to me afterwards to tell me how much they enjoyed the Roast.

ROAST FOR MIKE MILLER FOR HIS 65TH BIRTHDAY

I am very happy to be here to honor my good friend, Mike Miller. I've known Mike for over forty years, so I feel qualified to give some insights into who he really is and share with you some things about him that you may not have known.

I'm indeed honored to be speaking this evening. All of you should also feel sincerely honored, since at this event we'll have the opportunity to meet a person who deserves the respect and accolades of everyone here — a person of incredible charm and intelligence — a person of unquestioned integrity, honesty and capability, who has worked hard, accomplished much and is an outstanding example to all. But enough about Joan. Let's get on with a few words about Mike.

A few minutes ago, I spoke to some of Mike's friends, and they implored me to go easy on him. Let me assure you, that no matter how cruel the jokes may appear, no matter how vicious the insults may seem, no matter how embarrassing his exploits may sound, I am respecting their wishes and going easy on him.

I want you to remember that regardless of what I am about to say, Mike is a tremendous example to those young people who say, "I don't want an education; I don't want to work hard to achieve a good life; I don't want to be a responsible person." We can point to Mike and say to them, "If you don't change your attitudes, this is how you will turn out!"

When Mike was a bachelor, he liked to consider himself quite the ladies' man, but what you may not realize is that he focused on homeless women because he knew it was easier to talk to them into spending the night.

Mike has a prolific dating history. In fact, he's had so many blind dates, he qualified for a free seeing eye dog.

Mike is retired now, but he did have a few jobs during his working career. I remember once asking him why he left his last job. "A lot of reasons," said Mike. "The shoddy work, the vile language, the sloppiness, the inconsistent work hours — they just wouldn't put up with them anymore."

Once when Mike was preoccupied with his investment planning, it affected his job performance. His boss took note and said, "Mike, you don't seem to be yourself. What's the problem — ignorance or apathy?" Whereupon Mike said, "I don't know, and I don't care."

Of course, I can't talk about Mike without also including Joan, his loving wife of many years. When they were dating, Mike's mother asked him, "Why did you decide to go steady with Joan?" He replied that she was very different from all the other girls he had dated. "How so?" asked his mother. "She's the only one who ever agreed to a second date!" said Mike.

For Mike it was love at first sight. When they first met, Mike said, "Give me your phone number and I'll call you." Joan said, "It's in the book." Mike said, "Fine, what's your last name?" Joan said, "That's in the book too."

After the first few dates, Mike proposed marriage, saying that he stayed up all night thinking of her. Joan said, "Of course I love you, but why are you proposing to me so soon after we met?" Mike, always the romantic, replied, "I just gotta get some sleep."

But as they got to know each other, Joan also fell madly in love. In fact, on their third date, Mike took Joan to a Chinese restaurant and asked her how she liked her rice — boiled or fried? Joan said, "Thrown."

And so they were married and have shared a wonderful life together. To this day, Joan is always supportive of Mike.

Recently, Mike had a medical exam and the doctor said, "I don't like the looks of your husband, Mrs. Miller." Joan stuck right up for Mike and said, "Neither do I, but he's good to the children."

Why even tonight, an old friend commented that Mike doesn't seem to be dressing as well as he did 20 years ago. Joan immediately told him he must be mistaken, since Mike was wearing the exact same clothes.

I don't wish to imply that Mike is over the hill, but recently, they slipped away for a romantic second honeymoon. On the first night, Mike held Joan's hand and promptly fell asleep. The next night, the same thing happened. On the third night, when Mike reached for Joan's hand, she looked at him crossly and said, "Are you some kind of sex maniac? Three nights in a row!"

Recently, Mike asked Joan, "Will you love me when I'm old and feeble?" and Joan replied, "Of course I do."

Of course, with age and experience Mike has achieved much knowledge. Just recently, he was giving advice to the children. He told them that the two things necessary for a successful life were honesty and wisdom. Honesty means that no matter what happens, no matter what the cost, no matter how adversely it may affect you, always keep your word once you give it. The children understood that and then asked about wisdom. Mike said, "Never give your word."

I'd like to conclude by reading an Edgar Guest poem entitled, "A Friend".

A friend is one who takes your hand
And talks a speech you understand.
He's partly kindness, partly mirth
And faith unfaltering in your worth.

He's first to cheer you on success

And last to leave you in distress.

A friend is constant, honest, true.

In short, old pal, he's just like you.

Happy birthday, dear friend!

SAMPLE ROAST INTRODUCTIONS

The purpose of the Roast introduction is the same whether you are the Master of Ceremonies or one of the Roasters. It is to put the audience in a relaxed and cheerful mood for your presentation. A well-designed introduction should tell a little bit about yourself and your relationship to the person being Roasted. It can then describe in a humorous way why you were picked and why you accepted this honor. Last, but certainly not least, it should end with an appropriate (funny) lead-in to your Roast.

Some examples of good introductory material are as follows:

* Introducing other Roasters
    * In my book, our next speaker is eloquent, brilliant, and an all-around great person, but I only write fiction.
    * There are some speakers who need no introduction, but since John needs all the help he can get, let me tell you a little about him.
    * Some speakers are worth every penny they get paid, and that is certainly true of our next speaker since he is working for free.
    * Our next speaker offered to write his own introduction, but we couldn't let him, due to legal constraints. It's called TRUTH IN ADVERTISING.

* Our next speaker has been sought after for years. But enough about his outstanding arrest warrants', let's get on with the proceedings.

* Introducing your Roast

    * I spoke to David's family a few minutes ago and they implored me to go easy on him. Let me assure you all that no matter how cruel the jokes may appear, no matter how vicious the insults may seem, no matter how embarrassing his exploits may sound, I AM going easy on him.

    * I spoke with John's (or Linda's) children before dinner. They all said they always wanted to grow up to be just like their dad (or mom). After tonight, they may change their minds.

    * I've been to many of these events. I've seen people become the object of jokes without mercy, character assassinations without limit, and embarrassments beyond belief. I can honestly say that never in my life have I seen a Roastee who was so deserving of that kind of treatment.

    * I want you to remember that regardless of what I am about to say, John is a tremendous example to these young people who say, "I don't want to get educated," "I don't want to work hard to achieve a good life," "I don't want to be a responsible person." We can point to John and say to them, "If you don't change your

way of thinking and behaving, this is how you can turn out."

* Linda is a perfect example that if a person works hard, studies diligently, plays by the rules and follows a dream, it doesn't always work out.

* As you know, it is a tradition to Roast someone who has been an outstanding member of the community, who has achieved a great deal in both their personal and professional lives, and also can serve as a great role model to the younger generation. Tonight we totally break with tradition by honoring John.

* Ladies and gentlemen, at tonight's gathering we could honor a man whom everyone knows, a man who many look to for guidance, a man who is a perfect example of all that is good in a person, a man of unquestioned insight and moral integrity. But enough about the Pope. Let's get on with David's Roast.

* When asked to participate in tonight's Roast, I felt like Zsa Zsa Gabor's fifth husband on their honeymoon. I had a pretty good idea of what was expected of me, but had no idea of how to make it interesting.

SAMPLE ROAST SUBJECT MATERIAL

The basic essence of a Roast is to take some experience or characteristic and to incorporate it into a joke or story that pokes good natured fun at the person being Roasted, the Roastee. This may or may not actually be accurate with regard to the particular person being Roasted.

For example, let's assume that the Roastee is a very good piano player. The following story could be told. "Before John decided to concentrate on playing the piano, he tried the organ. But after a few weeks he had to give it up. The monkey ran away."

Now let's assume that the Roastee does not play a musical instrument. The story can be told as follows: "Most people don't know that when John was a young man, he very much wanted to play the organ. But after trying it for a few weeks, he had to give it up. The monkey ran away."

Another technique is to introduce a third party as the object of the joke. For example, one could say, "When John was a young man, he had a friend David who wanted to play the organ. But after a few weeks, he gave it up as the monkey ran away." Remember, the goal is to entertain. By using techniques like these, almost any material can be used to help create an enjoyable Roast.

The following are examples that you may find helpful, either as is or modified as appropriate. In order to help personalize this material, some names will be used. In most jokes and stories, male pronouns are used. This was done to use a simple and consistent format and can easily be adapted by the reader to apply to females as well. For easier reference, each example will be shown under the situation or category to which it generally applies.

Accountants

If an accountant's wife cannot sleep, what does she say? "Darling, could you tell me about your work?"

* * * * *

Early in his career, John was hired to replace the accountant who was retiring. Each and every morning the more experienced accountant began the day, by opening his desk drawer, taking out a worn envelope and removing a yellowing piece of paper. He reads it, nods his head, looks around the room with renewed vigor and returns the envelope to the drawer. Then begins his day's work.

John could hardly wait to see what was in the mysterious envelope that the soon to be retired accountant would look at each morning. John felt inadequate in replacing the far wiser and more highly esteemed accountant. Surely, he thinks to himself, it must contain the great secret to his success, a wondrous treasure of inspiration and motivation. His fingers trembled anxiously on the first day John took over his role as the company accountant. He removed the mysterious envelope from the drawer and reads the following message:

"Credits by the window,

Debits by the door."

* * * * *

David once received a call from a client who was furious about David's monthly statement. He accused David of being a greedy blood-sucker who was taking advantage of his clients. David listened intently and finally exploded, "You are such an ingrate. Who do you think I named my yacht after?"

* * * * *

David had just read the story of Cinderella to his young daughter for the first time. The little girl was fascinated by the story, especially the part where the pumpkin turns into a golden coach. Suddenly she piped up, "Daddy, when the pumpkin turned into a golden coach, would that be classed as income or a long-term capital gain?"

* * * * *

"How have you managed to buy such a luxurious villa while your income is so low?" asked the IRS auditor. "Well," John answered, "while fishing last summer, I had caught a large golden fish. When I took it off the hook, the fish opened his mouth and said, "I am a magical fish. Throw me back to the sea and I'll give you the most luxurious villa you have ever seen." "I threw the fish back to the sea and got the villa." "How can you prove such an unbelievable story?" "Well, you can see the villa, can't you?"

* * * * *

John went to a local bar where the owner was sure that his bartender was the strongest man around. The bar owner offered a standing $1,000.00 bet: The bartender would squeeze a lemon until all the juice ran into a glass and hand the lemon to a patron. Anyone who could squeeze one more drop of juice out would win the money. Many people had tried over time, but nobody could do it.

One day this scrawny little man came into the bar, wearing thick glasses and a polyester suit, and said in a tiny squeaky voice, "I'd like to try the bet." After the laughter had died down, the bartender said OK, grabbed a lemon and squeezed away. Then he handed the wrinkled remains of the rind to the little man. The crowd's laughter turned to total silence as the man clenched his fist around the lemon and six drops fell into the glass.

As the crowd cheered, the bartender paid the $1,000.00 and asked the little man, "What do you do for a living? Are you a lumberjack, a weight-lifter, or what?" The man replied, "I work for the IRS."

Aging

* John has reached the stage of life when his eyesight is starting to go. However, it doesn't bother him since he doesn't remember anything he sees anyway.

* What used to be his sex drive has turned into a putt.

* John was out walking and saw a small boy sitting on the curb crying. "What's the matter?" he asked. "I'm crying because I can't do what the big boys do," said the child. So John sat down and started crying also.

* I don't want to imply that John and Linda were over the hill when they got married, but on the first night of their honeymoon, John held Linda's hand and promptly fell asleep. The next night the same thing happened. On the third night when John reached for Linda's hand, Linda looked at him crossly and said, "Are you some kind of sex maniac … three nights in a row?!!"

* Just the other day, John asked Linda, "Will you love me when I'm old, feeble, and forgetful?" She immediately replied, "Of course I do."

* Everyone knows that it's natural to become forgetful as you grow older. But with John, it's become a crisis. Just last week, he woke up with a total hearing loss in his left ear. He quickly went to the emergency room. After a quick look, the doctor removed a suppository from the left ear. John said, "Thanks, Doc, now I know what I did with my hearing aid."

Bachelors

43

* A bachelor has no one to share his troubles with. But, then, why in the world would a bachelor have any troubles?

* When David was a bachelor, he invited Susan to his apartment to toast the new year with some fine imported champagne. But when she said, "It's only October," he said, "I don't like to do things at the last minute."

* When John was younger, he went to a computer dating service and specified that he was looking for someone who was petite, liked to dress formally, loved the water, was outgoing, enjoyed being with family, and was not very talkative. They set him up with a penguin.

* When Linda was dating, she met a fellow who told her his father owned a bank and his health was failing. Luckily, the relationship ended because she found out that his health was fine. It was the bank that was failing.

Consultants

A physician, a civil engineer and Dave were arguing about what was the oldest profession in the world.

The physician remarked, "Well, in the Bible, it says that God created Eve from a rib taken out of Adam. This clearly required surgery and so I can rightly claim that mine is the oldest profession in the world."

The civil engineer interrupted and said, "But even earlier in the book of Genesis, it states that God created the order of the heavens and the earth from out of the chaos. This was the first and certainly the most spectacular application of civil engineering. Therefore, fair doctor, you are wrong: mine is the oldest profession in the world."

Dave leaned back in his chair, smiled, and then said confidently, "Ah, but who do you think created the chaos?"

* * * * *

Top Ten Things You'll Never Hear From Your Consultant:
1. You're right; we're billing way too much for this.
2. Bet you I can go a week without saying "synergy" or "value-added".
3. How about paying us based on the success of the project?
4. This whole strategy is based on a Harvard business case I read.
5. Actually, the only difference is that we charge more than they do.
6. I don't know enough to speak intelligently about that.
7. Implementation? I only care about writing long reports.
8. I can't take the credit. It was Ed in your marketing department.

9. The problem is, you have too much work for too few people.

10. Everything looks okay to me. You really don't need me.

* * * * *

Consulting is a wonderful business. They ask you questions in the guise of research; then come back and sell you the information you gave them.

Courtship and Dating

* Early in their relationship, a friend asked John how things were progressing with his courtship of Susan. He said, "Great! Last night she told me she had said no for the last time."

* When Linda received her engagement ring, she waved her ring finger profusely. She tried to model and display it as conspicuously as possible, but no one seemed to notice it. Finally, she blurted out, "I'm really uncomfortable. I'm so warm in my new diamond ring."

* A friend of Linda's went to a computer dating service and said she wanted a man who had good character and loved his family. She did not care about looks, profession, or wealth. Later, a man came in and requested a woman with intelligence. He said he didn't

care about anything else. The computer matched them up because they had so much in common —- LYING.

* When John was dating, he treated his dates like royalty. He took them to Burger King and Dairy Queen.

* Susan had to turn down a marriage proposal when she was a young woman. She lived on 76th Street and he lived on 49th Street and her mother had told her she should never marry anyone beneath her station.

Golf

* When John was a young man, he was dating a young lady. Being the forthright person we all know he is, he told her that although he liked her, she must be aware of the fact that he loved golf. Golf was his passion and it would always take first priority. "That's all right," she said. "But since you are being so honest with me, I feel that I should also come clean and let you know that I am a hooker." "Maybe you're not keeping your left arm straight on your back swing," said John.

* For eighteen holes, David's caddy had been snickering and nodding his head in disappointment after just about every shot he took. Finally, David lost his temper and said, "You must be the worst caddy in the world!" The caddy grinned and said, "That, sir, would be too great a coincidence."

* David came running up just in time to join his friends on the first tee. "Since it's Sunday, we didn't think you would make it," one said. "Well, it was a toss of the coin between playing golf and going to church." "So, why are you so late?" asked one of his friends. "I had to toss the coin twenty times."

Jewish Humor

* 5,759 years according to Jewish calendar

  4,696 years according to Chinese calendar

  1,063 total number of years that Jews went without Chinese food.

* What did the waiter ask the group of dining Jewish mothers?

  "Is ANYTHING all right?"

* How many Jewish mothers does it take to change a light bulb?

  (Sigh) Don't bother; I'll sit in the dark. I don't want to be a nuisance to anybody.

* Sam Levy was driving down the road, gets pulled over by a policeman. Walking up to Sam's car, the policeman says, "Your wife fell out of the car 5 miles back." Sam replies, "Thank God for that … I'd thought I'd gone deaf!"

* Short summary of every Jewish holiday: "They tried to kill us, we won, let's eat."

* Did you hear about the bum who walked up to the Jewish mother on the street and said, "Lady, I haven't eaten in three days."

"Force yourself," she replied.

* What's the difference between a Rottweiler and a Jewish Mother?

Eventually, the Rottweiler lets go.

* A young Jewish man calls his mother and says, "Mom, I'm bringing home a wonderful woman I want to marry. She's a Native American and her name is Shooting Star."

"How nice," says his mother.

"I have an Indian name too," he says. "It's Running Water" and you have to call me that from now on."

"How nice," says his mother.

"You have to have an Indian name too, mom," he says.

"I already do," says the mother. "Just call me Sitting Shiva."

* A man calls his mother in Florida. "Mom, how are you?"

"Not too good," says the mother. "I've been very weak."

The son says, "Why are you so weak?"

She says, "Because I haven't eaten in 38 days."

The man says, "That's terrible. Why haven't you eaten in 38 days?"

The mother answers, "Because I didn't want my mouth to be filled with food if you should call."

* Jewish view on when life begins: There's a big controversy on when life begins. In Jewish tradition, the fetus is not considered viable until after it graduates from medical school.

* A Jewish boy comes home from school and tells his mother he's been given a part in the school play. "Wonderful. What part is it?" The boy says, "I play the part of the Jewish husband." The mother scowls and says, "Go back and tell the teacher you want a speaking part.

* Jewish telegram: "Begin worrying. Details to follow."

Judges

Judge John, being a family man himself, had a soft heart and agreed to let the man go free, since he was only trying to feed his starving family and it was his first and only offense and a misdemeanor at that. Killing an endangered species. He said he was sitting on the beach, tossing stones into the water and didn't see the Snowy Egret fly by.

"Before you go, though, I want to ask you a question," interposed Judge John. "What does Egret taste like?"

"Well your Honor," the man told him, "it has the taste between California condor and a Bald Eagle!"

* * * * *

One of the more noteworthy cases that came through David's courtroom was the following:

A young woman was appearing in court to face a public disorder charge. After the charges were read, she was asked how she pleaded. "Not guilty," the woman answered emphatically.

The prosecutor then approached the woman and said, "Is it true that on the 11th of December last year, you committed an act of gross indecency with a one-legged dwarf who was waving a flag on the roof of a car, while traveling at over 100 mph through the center of Los Angeles, in the middle of a rainstorm?"

The woman composed herself, looked straight at the prosecutor and calmly said, "What was the date again?"

* * * * *

A prosecuting attorney called his first witness, a grandmotherly, elderly woman, to the stand. He approached her and asked, "Mrs. Jones, do you know me?"

She responded, "Why, yes, I do know you Mr. Johnson. I've known you since you were a young boy. And frankly, you've been a big disappointment to me. You lie, you cheat on your wife, you manipulate people and talk about them behind their backs. You think you're a rising big shot when you haven't the brains to realize you never will amount to anything more than a two-bit paper pusher. Yes, I know you."

The lawyer was stunned. Not knowing what else to do, he pointed across the room and asked, "Mrs. Williams, do you know the defense attorney?"

She again replied, "Why, yes I do. I've known Mr. Bradley since he was a youngster, too. I used to baby-sit him for his parents. And he, too, has been a real disappointment to me. He's lazy, bigoted, and has a drinking problem. The man can't build a normal relationship with anyone, and his law practice is one of the shoddiest in the entire state. Yes, I know him."

At this point, the judge rapped the courtroom to silence and called both attorneys to the bench. In a very quiet voice, he said with menace, "If either of you asks her if she knows me, you'll be jailed for contempt!"

Lawyers

John, an M.D. and a lawyer friend were attending a cocktail party when the M.D. was approached by a man who asked advice on how to handle his ulcer. The doctor mumbled some medical advice, then turned to the lawyer and asked, "How do you handle the situation when you are asked for advice during a social function?"

"Just bill the patient for such advice," replied the lawyer.

On the next morning, the doctor arrived at his office and issued the ulcer-stricken man a $50.00 invoice. That afternoon, he received a $100.00 invoice from the lawyer.

* * * * *

A new client had just come in to see David, a well known attorney. "Can you tell me how much you charge?" said the client.

"Of course," the lawyer replied, "I charge $200.00 to answer three questions!"

"Well, that's a bit steep, isn't it?"

"Yes it is," said the lawyer, "And what's your third question?"

* * * * *

"I'm beginning to think that my lawyer is too interested in making money."

"Why do you say that?"

"Listen to this from his bill: 'For waking up at night and thinking about your case: $25.00'."

* * * * *

The lawyer's son wanted to follow in his father's footsteps, so he went to law school. He graduated with honors and then went home to join his father's firm. At the end of his first day at work, he rushed into his father's office and said, "Father, father, in one day, I settled the accident case that you've been working on for ten years!"

His father responded, "You idiot, we lived on the funding of that case for ten years!"

* * * * *

A lawyer, who was talking to his son about entering college, said, "What got into your head that you want to be a doctor instead of a lawyer?"

"Well, dad," answered the son, "did you ever hear anybody get up in a crowd and shout frantically, 'Is there a lawyer in the house?'"

* * * * *

What's the difference between a good lawyer and a bad lawyer?

A bad lawyer can let a case drag out for several years. A good lawyer can make it last even longer.

* * * * *

A lawyer opened the door of his BMW, when suddenly, a car came along and hit the door, ripping it off completely. When the police arrived at the scene, the lawyer was complaining bitterly about the damage to his precious BMW. "Officer, look what they've done to my Beeeemer!!!", he whined.

"You lawyers are so materialistic, you make me sick!!!" retorted the officer. "You're so worried about your stupid BMW, that you didn't even notice that your left arm was ripped off!!!"

"Oh my gaaad ...," replied the lawyer, finally noticing the bloody left shoulder where his arm once was. "Where's my Rolex???!!!!!"

* * * * *

The day after a verdict had been entered against his client, John rushed to the judge's chambers, demanding that the case be reopened, saying, "I have new evidence that makes a huge difference in my client's defense." The judge asked, "What new evidence could you have?" The lawyer replied, "My client has an extra $10,000.00 and I just found out about it!"

* * * * *

How many lawyers does it take to change a light bulb?

"How many can you afford?"

It only takes one to change your bulb ... to his.

Two. One to change it and one to keep interrupting by standing up and shouting "Objection!"

Three. One to do it and two to sue him for malpractice.

Three. One to turn the bulb, one to shake him off the ladder and the third to sue the ladder company.

Three. One to sue the power company for insufficiently supplying power, or negligent failure to prevent the surge that made the bulb burn out in the first place, one to sue the electrician who wired the house and one to sue the bulb manufacturers.

Fifty four. Eight to argue, one to get a continuance, one to object, one to demur, two to research precedents, one to dictate a letter, one to stipulate, five to turn in their time cards, one to depose, one to write interrogatories, two to settle, one to order a secretary to change the bulb and twenty-eight to bill for professional services.

Nurses

As you all know, Linda has been a terrific nurse for many years. This is one of her favorite stories:

"Three nurses went to heaven and were awaiting their turn with St. Peter to plead their case to enter the pearly gates.

The first nurse said, "I worked in an emergency room. We tried our best to help patients, but occasionally, we did lose one. I think I deserve to go to heaven." St. Peter looks at her file and admits her to heaven.

The second nurse says, "I worked in an operating room. It's a very high stress environment and we do our best. Sometimes the patients are too sick and we lose them, but overall, we try very hard." St. Peter looks at her file and admits her to heaven.

The third nurse says, "I was a case manager for an HMO." St. Peter looks at her file. He pulls out a calculator and starts punching away at it furiously, constantly going back to the nurse's file. After a few minutes, St. Peter looks up, smiles, and says, "Congratulations! You've been admitted to heaven … for five days!"

* * * * *

Susan was once making rounds with a nurse trainee. When they got to the first bed, the patient was laying half dead. "Did you give this man two tablets every eight hours?" asks the doctor.

"Oh, no," replies the nurse, "I gave him eight tablets every two hours!"

At the next bed, the next patient also appears half dead. "Nurse, did you give this man one tablet every twelve hours?"

"Oops, I gave him twelve tablets every one hour," replied the nurse.

Unfortunately, at the next bed, the patient was howling with pain. "Nurse, did you prick his boil?"

"Oh my goodness!" replies the nurse.

Pharmacists

One of Dave's customers went for an interview for a job as a TV news broadcaster. The interview went quite well, but the trouble was, he kept winking and stammering.

The interviewer said, "Although you have a lot of the qualities we're looking for, the fact that you keep winking and stammering disqualifies you."

"Oh, that's no problem," said the man. "If I take a couple of aspirin, I stop winking and stammering for an hour."

"Show me," said the interviewer.

So the man reached into his pocket. Embarrassingly, he pulled out loads of condoms of every variety — ribbed, flavored, colored and everything else before he found the packet of aspirin. He took the aspirin and soon talked perfectly and stopped winking and stammering.

The interviewer said, "That's amazing, but I don't think we could employ someone who'd be womanizing all over the country."

"Excuse me!" exclaimed the man, "I'm a happily married man, not a womanizer!"

"Well, how do you explain all the condoms, then?" asked the interviewer.

The man replied, "Have you ever gone into a drug store, stammering and winking, and asked for a packet of aspirin?"

* * * * *

One of Jim's friends goes to a travel agent and books a two week cruise for himself and his girlfriend. A couple days before the cruise, the travel agent calls and says the cruise has been canceled, but he can get them on a three day cruise instead. The guy says, "OK," and goes to the drug store to buy three Dramamine and three condoms.

The next day, the agent calls back and says he now can book a five day cruise. The guy says he'll take it. He returns to the same drug store and buys two more Dramamine and two more condoms.

The following day, the travel agent calls again and says he can now book an eight day cruise. The guy says, "OK," and goes back to the drug store and asks for three more Dramamine and three more condoms.

Finally, the pharmacist asks, "Look, if it makes you that sick, how come you keep doing it?"

Programmers

Remember when an application was for employment

A program was a TV show

A cursor used profanity

A keyboard was a piano!

Memory was something that you lost with age

A CD was a bank account

And if you had a 3 1/2 inch floppy

You hoped nobody found out!

Compress was something you did to garbage

Not something you did to a file

And if you unzipped anything in public

You'd be in jail for awhile!

59

Log on was adding wood to a fire

Hard drive was a long trip on the road

A mouse pad was where a mouse lived

And a back-up happened to your commode!

Cut - you did with a pocket knife

Paste you did with glue

A web was a spider's home

And a virus was the flu!

I guess I'll stick to my pad and paper

And the memory in my head

I hear nobody's been killed in a computer crash

But when it happens, they wish they were dead!

* * * * *

David was walking along the beach when he found a lamp. Upon rubbing the lamp, a genie appeared who stated, "I am the most powerful genie in the world. I can grant you any wish you want, but only one wish."

David thought and said, "I have always wanted a road from Hawaii to California since I don't like to fly." The genie responded that the effort to put in the pilings and the amount of concrete is a job that even a genie can't easily perform in enough time to complete the job within David's lifetime.

David then said, "Well, I am a programmer and my programs have a lot of users. Please make all the users satisfied with my programs and let them ask for sensible changes."

The genie paused, sighed and asked, "Two lanes or four?"

* * * * *

John said to his son, "Here, I brought you a new basketball."
"Thank you, daddy, but where is the user's guide?"

Psychologists and Doctors

Once John met a colleague at their twentieth college reunion. John looked like he just graduated, while his friend looked old, worried and withered. The older looking one asks the other, "What's your secret?" Listening to other people's problems every day, all day long, for years on end, has made an old man of me."

John replies, "Who listens?"

* * * * *

Some interesting problems are brought to John by his patients:
Doctor, doctor, I keep thinking I am a set of curtains!
Pull yourself together, man!
Doctor, doctor, I keep thinking I'm a bell.
Well, just go home and if the feeling persists, give me a ring.
Doctor, doctor, people tell me I'm a wheelbarrow.

61

Don't let people push you around.

Doctor, doctor, I can't concentrate. One minute I'm OK and the next minute, I'm blank!

And how long have you had this complaint?

What complaint?

Doctor, doctor, I can't stop stealing things.

Take these pills for a week. If that doesn't work, I would like to have a color TV.

Doctor, doctor, I keep thinking I'm a spoon.

Sit there and don't stir.

Doctor, doctor, I'm manic-depressive.

Calm down. Cheer up. Clam down. Cheer up. Calm …

Doctor, doctor, I keep trying to get into fights.

And how long have you had this complaint?

Who wants to know?

* * * * *

John has a knack for diagnosis of strange symptoms:

A man walks into John's office. He has a cucumber up his nose, a carrot in his left ear and a banana in his right ear. What's the matter with me?" he asks the doctor.

John replies, "You're not eating properly."

"Doctor, are you sure I'm suffering from pneumonia?" asked one of John's patients. "I've heard once about a doctor treating someone with pneumonia and finally he died of typhus."

"Don't worry," John assured him. "If I treat someone with pneumonia, he will die of pneumonia."

Sales Persons

A woman is undressing for a bath and while she's standing naked, there's a knock at the door. The woman calls, "Who is it?"

A voice answers, "A blind salesman."

The woman decides to get a thrill by having the blind man in the room while she's naked, so she lets him in. The man walks in, looks straight at her and says, "Uhhhh, well, hello there. Can I sell you a blind, or perhaps curtains?"

* * * * *

Sales people are always fair game for jokes and stories like these:

A salesman walking along the beach found a bottle. When he rubbed it, lo and behold, a genie appeared.

"I will grant you three wishes," announced the genie. "But since Satan still hates me, for every wish you make, your rival gets the wish as well — only double."

The salesman thought about this for awhile. "For my first wish, I would like ten million dollars," he announced.

Instantly, the genie gave him a Swiss bank account number and assured the man that $10,000,000 had been deposited. "But your rival has just received $20,000,000," the genie said.

"I've always wanted a Ferrari," the salesman said.

63

Instantly, a Ferrari appeared. "But your rival has just received two Ferraris," the genie said. "And what is your last wish?"

"Well," said the salesman, "I've always wanted to donate a kidney for transplant."

* * * * *

A salesman's pitch started with, "This computer will cut your workload by 50%."

The customer responded, "That's great. I'll take two of them."

* * * * *

A salesman who was out on his territory had a heart attack in his motel room and died. The motel manager called the salesman's company and relayed the tragedy to the salesman's boss.

The boss received the news in a nonchalant manner and told the motel manager, "Please return his samples by UPS and search his pants for orders."

Waiters

John was visiting a resort in the Mojave Desert and while driving around the desert, his car ran out of gas. Although he knew he should wait for help to save him, he panicked and decided to walk out of the desert. After a couple of hours under the blazing sun, he spied a shack in the distance. He made his way to the shack and found it was a small discount necktie shop. He entered and asked the proprietor for some water, but was told that they sold neckties and weren't in business to save travelers who violated the cardinal rule of the desert — take water with you and don't leave your car. But the fellow directed him to a restaurant located in an oasis about 5 miles away. Against his better judgment, John set off in the direction indicated. John was lucky and found the restaurant. Barely being able to walk, he entered the restaurant, only to be confronted by the maitre de. John asked for water and told the fellow of his bad luck. The maitre de looked disdainfully at him and said, "You must wear a necktie at our restaurant."

<u>Some Waiter Questions and Answers:</u>

Waiter, what's this fly doing in my soup?

Um, looks to me to be backstroke, sir …

Waiter, waiter, do you have frog's legs?

Certainly, sir!

Well, hop over here and get me a sandwich!

* * * * *

Waiter, there's a fly in my soup!

No sir, that's a cockroach. The fly is on your steak.

Waiter, there's dirt in my soup. What does this mean?

If you want your fortune told, go find a gypsy.

Waiter, how long do I have to wait for a table?

Two hours or a twenty, whichever comes first.

Waiter, there's a fly in my soup!

Surely not, sir. It must be one of those vitamin bees you hear so much about.

Waiter, I'd like a cup of coffee, please, with no cream.

I'm sorry, sir, but we're out of cream. How about with no milk?

Waiter, this coffee tastes like dirt!

Yes sir, that's because it was only ground this morning.

Waiter, I can't seem to find any oysters in this oyster soup.

Would you expect to find angels in angel cake?

General and Miscellaneous *(These have a wide use for almost any situation)*

Larry's barn burned down and his wife, Susan, called the insurance company. Susan told the insurance company, "We had that barn insured for fifty thousand and I want my money." The agent replied, "Whoa there, just a minute, Susan. Insurance doesn't work quite like that. We will ascertain the value of what was insured and provide you with a new one of comparable worth." After a long pause, Susan said, "Then I'd like to cancel the policy on my husband."

* * * * *

Late one night in Washington, D.C., a mugger jumped a well-dressed man, gun to his ribs. "Give me your money!" he demanded. The man stiffened, but said indignantly, "You can't do this to me —

I'm a U.S. Congressman!" "In that case," replied the robber, "give me my money!"

* * * * *

A man and his wife were in a fancy restaurant. While ordering, they noticed the waiter had a spoon in his shirt pocket, and after looking around, they observed the other waiters and busboys each had a similar spoon. So the husband says, "What's with the spoon?"

The waiter said, "Well, we had this company come in and evaluate our time management and they found that people drop their spoon 74.8% more often than any other utensil. So if we carry one with us, we can reduce the trips back to the kitchen by 3 hours per shift."

The husband was impressed. Sure enough, he dropped his spoon during dining and the waiter replaced it with his, stating, "I'll just get another when I go to the kitchen for something else."

While ordering dessert, the husband noted that the waiter had a very thin string hanging from the fly of his pants, as did the other waiters, so the husband asked, "Hey, there's a string on your pants."

The waiter tells him, "Not all my customers are as observant as you … the same company found that we can reduce the amount of time spent in the bathroom by 2 hours each shift if we tie a string around the end of you-know-what, and when we have to go, we just unzip and pull it out with the string completely eliminating the need to wash up and saving time."

The husband was impressed, but asked, "It's a good idea, but how do you get it back in your pants?"

The waiter leaned close and whispered, "Well, I don't know about the rest of them, but personally I use the spoon."

* * * * *

A man is in bed with his wife when there is a knock at the door. He rolls over, looks at his clock, and it's 3:30 in the morning. "I'm not getting out of bed at this time," he thinks, and rolls over.

Then a louder knock follows. "Aren't you going to answer that?" says his wife. So he drags himself out of bed and goes downstairs. He opens the door and there is a man standing on the porch. It didn't take the homeowner long to realize the man was drunk.

"Hi there," slurs the stranger. "Can you give me a push?"

"No, get lost! It's half past three. I was in bed," says the man and he slams the door. He goes back up to bed and tells his wife what happened and she says, "That wasn't very nice of you. Remember that night we broke down in the pouring rain on the way to pick the kids up from the babysitter and you had to knock on that man's house to get us started again? What would have happened if he'd told us to get lost?"

"But the guy was drunk," says the husband. "It doesn't matter," says the wife. "He needs our help and it would be the right thing to help him."

So the husband gets out of bed again, gets dressed, and goes downstairs. He opens the front door, and not being able to see the stranger anywhere, he shouts out, "Hey, do you still want a push?" And he hears a voice cry out, "Yeah, please." But still being unable to see the stranger, he shouts, "Where are you?"

And the drunk replies, "Over here, on the swing."

* * * * *

Murphy, a dishonest lawyer, bribed one of his client's jurors to hold out for a charge of manslaughter, fearing the murder charge being brought by the state. They were out for days before returning with the verdict: manslaughter!!

Later, as Murphy paid off the corrupt juror, he asked him if he had a hard time convincing the other jurors to see things his way.

"Boy, did I!" said the juror. "They kept voting to acquit!"

* * * * *

A woman decides to have a facelift for her birthday. She spends $5,000 and feels pretty good about the results. On her way home, she stops at a newsstand to buy a paper. Before leaving, she asks the sales clerk, "I hope you don't mind my asking, but how old do you think I am?"

"About 32," the clerk replies.

"I'm actually 47," the woman says happily.

A little while later, she goes into McDonald's, and upon getting her order, asks the counter girl the same question. She replies, "I'd guess about 29."

The woman replies, "Nope, I am 47." Now she is feeling really good about herself.

While waiting for the bus home, she asks an old man the same question. He replies, "I'm 78 and my eyesight is starting to go. Although, when I was young, there was a sure way to tell how old a woman was, but it requires you to let me put my hands up your shirt and feel your breasts. Then I can tell exactly how old you are."

They waited in silence on the empty street until curiosity got the best of the woman, and she finally said, "What the hell, go ahead."

The old man slips both hands up her shirt, under her bra, and begins to feel around. After a couple of minutes, she says, "Okay, okay, how old am I?"

He removes his hands and says, "You are 47."

Stunned, the woman says, "How did you know?" The old man replies, "I was behind you in line at McDonald's."

* * * * *

Three men stand before St. Peter awaiting admission into Heaven. However, St. Peter has been informed that Heaven will only admit 33% of applicants today. The admissions standard: Who died the worst death? So, St. Peter takes each of the three men aside in turn and asks them about how they died.

First man: "I'd been suspecting for a long time that my wife was cheating on me. I decided to come home early from work one afternoon and check to see if I could catch her in the act. When I got back to my apartment, I heard the water running. My wife was in the shower. I looked everywhere for the guy, but couldn't find anyone or any trace that he had been there. The last place I looked was out on the balcony.

I found the SOB hanging from the edge, trying to get back in! So I started jumping up and down on his hands, and he yelled, but he didn't fall. So I ran inside and got a hammer, and crushed his fingers with it until he fell twenty-five floors screaming in agony. But the fall didn't kill him. He landed in some bushes! So I dragged the refrigerator from the kitchen (it weighed about a ton), pulled it to the balcony, and hurled it over the edge. It landed right on the guy and killed him. But then I felt so horrible about what I had done, I went back into the bedroom and shot myself."

St. Peter nodded slowly as the man recounted the story. Then, telling the first man to wait, he took the second aside.

Second man: "I lived on the twenty-seventh floor of this apartment building. I had just purchased this book on morning exercises and was practicing them on my balcony, enjoying the sunshine, when I lost my balance and fell off the edge. Luckily, I only fell about two floors before grabbing another balcony and holding on for dear life. I was trying to pull myself up when this guy came running onto what must been his balcony and started jumping up and down on my hands. I screamed in pain, but he seemed really irate.

When he finally stopped, I tried to pull myself up again, but he came out with a hammer and smashed my fingers to a pulp! I fell, and I thought I was dead, but I landed in some bushes. I couldn't believe my second stroke of luck, but it didn't last. The last thing I saw was this enormous refrigerator falling from the building down on top of me and crushing me."

St. Peter comforted the man, who seemed to have several broken bones. Then he told him to wait, and turned to the third man.

Third man: "Picture this. You're hiding, naked, in a refrigerator …"

* * * * *

A secretary was leaving the office one Friday evening when she encountered Mr. Jones, the Human Resources manager, standing in front of a shredder with a piece of paper in his hand.

"Listen," said Mr. Jones, "this is important and my secretary has already left. Can you make this thing work?"

"Certainly," said the secretary. She turned the machine on, inserted the paper, and pressed the start button.

"Excellent, excellent!" said Mr. Jones as his paper disappeared inside the shredder. "I just need one copy."

* * * * *

A man is hired by the circus to perform a necessary, but rather unpleasant task. He is asked to walk behind the elephants in the center ring, shoveling aside their droppings as they walk about. After a rather difficult evening at work, he goes to the circus cafeteria, sits with other workers, and begins complaining about his work.

"It's just terrible work, walking behind those huge beasts and first dodging, then shoveling aside the dung they produce. My arms are tired, my shoes and pants are a mess, and I'll have to shower before I return home, because of the stink."

His friends at work agree: "Why don't you just quit this miserable job and find something more rewarding to do? You have to have some skills and talents that you can put to use somewhere else."

He looks at them, stunned: "You know, you're probably right, but I just can't give up the glamour of show business!"

* * * * *

Andy wants a job as a signalman on the railways. He is told to meet the inspector at the signal box. The inspector puts this question to him: "What would you do if you realized that two trains were heading for each other on the same track?"

Andy says, "I would switch the points for one of the trains."

"What if the lever broke?" asked the inspector.

"Then I'd dash down out of the signal box," said Andy, "and I'd use the manual lever over there."

"What if that had been struck by lightning?"

73

"Then," Andy continues, "I'd run back into the signal box and phone the next signal box."

"What if the phone was engaged?"

"Well, in that case," persevered Andy, "I'd rush down out of the box and use the public emergency phone at the level crossing up there."

"What if that was vandalized?"

"Oh, well, then I'd run into the village and get my Uncle Silas."

This puzzles the inspector, so he asks, "Why would you do that?"

Came the answer, "Because he's never seen a train crash."

* * * * *

Three boys are in the school yard bragging of how great their fathers are.

The first one says: "Well, my father runs the fastest. He can fire an arrow and start to run. I tell you, he gets there before the arrow."

The second one says: "Ha! You think that's fast! My father is a hunter. He can shoot his gun and be there before the bullet."

The third one listens to the other two and shakes his head. He then says, "You two know nothing about fast. My father is a civil servant. He stops working at 4:30 and he is home by 3:45!!"

* * * * *

*   Old accountants never die, they just lose their balance.

* Old actuaries never die, they just get broken down by age and sex.
* Old chemists never die, they just fail to react.
* Old doctors never die, they just lose their patience.
* Old electricians never die, they just lose contact.
* Old lawyers never die, they just lose their appeal.
* Old mathematicians never die, they just lose some of their functions.
* Old professors never die, they just lose their faculties.
* Old programmers never die, they just branch to a new address.
* Old publishers never die, they just go out of print.
* Old statisticians never die, they just become non-significant.

WISDOM AND QUESTIONS

1. "Don't sweat the petty things and don't pet the sweaty things."

2. "One tequila, two tequila, three tequila, floor."

3. "Atheism is a nonprophet organization."

4. "If man evolved from monkeys and apes, why do we still have monkeys and apes?"

5. "The main reason Santa is so jolly is because he knows where all the bad girls live."

6. "I went to a bookstore and asked the saleswoman, 'Where's the self-help section?' She said if she told me, it would defeat the purpose."

7. "Could it be that all those trick-or-treaters wearing sheets aren't going as ghosts but as mattresses?"

8. "If a mute swears, does his mother wash his hands with soap?"

9. "If a man is standing in the middle of the forest speaking and there is no woman around to hear him, is he still wrong?"

10. "Is there another word for synonym?"

11. "Isn't it a bit unnerving that doctors call what they do 'practice'?"

12. "Where do forest rangers go 'to get away from it all?'"

13. "What do you do when you seen an endangered animal eating an endangered plant?"

14. "If a parsley farmer is sued, can they garnish his wages?"

15. "Would a fly without wings be called a walk?"

16. "Why do they lock gas stations bathrooms? Are they afraid someone will use them?"

17. "If a turtle doesn't have a shell, is he homeless or naked?"

18. "Why don't sheep shrink when it rains?"

19. "Can vegetarians eat animal crackers?"

20. "If the police arrest a mime, do they tell him he has the right to remain silent?"

21. "Why do they put Braille on the drive-through bank machines?"

22. "How do they get deer to cross at that yellow road sign?"

23. "Is it true that cannibals don't eat clowns because they taste funny?"

PHILOSOPHICAL GEMS

1. "The lesser of two evils is still evil."

2. "Two wrongs don't make a right. But three rights make a left."

3. "The more things change ... the more different they become."

4. "A blank page cannot be read."

5. "A book does not end until the last page."

6. "A change of heart can be very painful."

7. "A couple alike is two of a kind."

8. "A detour demands a change."

9. "A friend in need wants something."

10. "A journey is getting from here to there."

11. "A secret is a fact not widely recognized."

12. "A space unfilled continues in emptiness."

13. "A thought goes without saying."

14. "A thought is an idea from within."

15. "Actuality is a matter of fact."

16. "An open secret is private only in name."

17. "An unsolved mystery leaves much in question."

18. "As we watch the parade we are its spectators."

19. "At life's beginning you are on its threshold."

20. "At the edge one has the choice to stand or fall."

21. "At this point you are thus far — and no farther."

22. "Capture a fleeting thought, and give birth to an idea."

23. "Dreams are thoughts you have in your sleep."

24. "Feeling good brings forth happiness."

25. "He who assaults you extends a personal attack."

26. "He who attempts a marathon is in for the long run."

27. "He who builds also creates."

28. "He who comes in first is not last unless he is the only one."

29. "He who has abundant chances has ample opportunity."

30. "He who is prepared to answer has a ready response."

31. "He who is speaking the truth does not talk falsely."

32. "He who speaks the truth uses words of wisdom."

33. "If the facts are revealed, then the truth be known."

34. "In order to choose, there must be more than one."

35. "In quietude silence reigns supreme."

36. "Infinity's end is out of reach."

37. "It is unless it is not."

38. "It stands to reason that things can be figured out."

39. "Letters are the elements of language."

40. "Life is for the living."

41. "Man's best friend likes him."

42. "Nothing can exist within a void."

43. "Once it can go no more, that's as far as it goes."

44. "Once the initial steps have been taken, the journey has begun."

45. "One cannot intentionally have an accident."

46. "One cannot live in the past."

47. "One who eats his words has food for thought."

48. "One who finds it can take it or leave it."

49. "One who has both feet on the ground has a foundation."

50. "One who has wisdom, knows."

51. "One who is behind the scenes is not noticed."

52. "One who is in the spot has found a place to be."

53. "One who is lost knows not where he is."

54. "One who speaks the facts has truth to tell."

55. "One who strains every nerve is surely anxious."

56. "Out of the mouth of babes comes sounds."

57. "Songs present the message they convey."

58. "Success comes from a lack of failure."

59. "Tag is a game of touch and go."

60. "That which is caged is kept within limits."

61. "That which is dead cannot grow."

62. "The absence of life is the presence of death."

63. "The all mighty dollar is worth itself in change."

64. "The clocks of the world have many faces."

65. "The missing link breaks the chain."

66. "The naked truth is exposed to all."

67. "The old way changes when a new one takes its place."

68. "The scales of justice weigh good and ill."

69. "The select few are chosen."

70. "The supreme moment can be no better."

71. "There are many varieties of people, all with humanness in common."

72. "To be a blacksmith is to go at it hammer and tongs."

73. "To be a statute is to have a heart of stone."

74. "To be confused is to have uncertainty."

75. "To be there is not to be there, unless there is here."

76. "To be in control of oneself is to be one's own master."

77. "To be in line one must follow another."

78. "Be last but not least is to be more than one before you."

79. "To be surrounded is to be within."

80. "To be unsatisfied is to leave much to be desired."

81. "To be warned is to receive the message."

82. "To be worthless is to be good for nothing."

83. "To carry a burden is to feel its weight."

84. "To choose one is to deny the other."

85. "To easily understand is to know the simple truth."

86. "To go the way you want is a step in the right direction."

87. "To hate yourself is to be one's own worst enemy."

88. "To have acquaintances is to know others."

89. "To have cold blood is not to be human."

90. "To hope for another is wishful thinking."

91. "To keep the ball rolling takes effort."

92. "To keep to oneself is to know no others."

93. "To know a language is to know its words."

94. "To know the meaning one must understand."

95. "To know where one stands is not to be lost."

96. "To look in the mirror is to see oneself."

97. "To look out is to see what is before you."

98. "To make oneself indispensable to everyone is to be all things to all men."

99. "To proclaim from rooftops is to risk a fall."

100. "To pull one's weight is to shoulder the burden."

101. "To put one's best foot forward is to have the other behind."

102. "To read between the lines is to see space."

103. "To search is to look, but yet not find."

104. "To see eye to eye is to look at another."

105. "To touch the flame is to know that it's lit."

106. "To see the glorious end one must be at the grand finale."

107. "To see with one's own eyes is not to be blind."

108. "To sell one's soul is to make a deal."

109. "To shed more light on the subject is to see it better."

110. "To sit on the fence, one needs balance."

111. "To some, your first breath is the beginning of the end."

112. "To win is not to lose."

113. "War is a bloody matter."

114. "What separates us from them is difference."

115. "When all is said and done, there is silence."

116. "When all the pieces fit, the puzzle is complete."

117. "When everything has been taken into account, all things have been considered."

118. "When the worst has happened, it can only get better."

119. "When things go from bad to worse, they are not getting better."

120. "Words of general meaning are words to that effect."

121. "Worry is a disturbance of the mind."

122. "You will know when you figure it out."

123. "Books and friends should be few but good."

124. "A friend in need is a friend indeed."

125. "A hedge between keeps friendship green."

126. "Love is blind; friendship closes its eyes."

127. "Do not use a hatchet to remove a fly from your friend's forehead."

128. "To have a friend, be a friend."

129. "The death of a friend is equivalent to the loss of a limb."

130. "Life without a friend is like death without a witness."

131. "The best mirror is an old friend."

132. "A cheerful friend is like a sunny day spreading brightness all around."

133. "There are many types of ships. There are wooden ships, plastic ships, and metal ships. But the best and most important types of ships are friendships."

134. "The only unsinkable ship is FRIENDSHIP."

135. "A friend is one to whom one may pour out all the contents of one's heart, chaff and grain together, knowing that the gentlest of hands will take and sift it, keep what is worth keeping and with a breath of kindness blow the rest away."

136. "It is better to be in chains with friends, than to be in a garden with strangers."

137. "Friends are the sunshine of life."

138. "No man is a failure who has friends."

139. "Friendship improves happiness and abates misery by doubling our joy and dividing our grief."

140. "In loneliness, in sickness, in confusion — the mere knowledge of friendship makes it possible to endure, even if the friend is powerless to help. It is enough that they exist. Friendship is not diminished by distance or time, by imprisonment or war, by suffering or silence. It is in these things that it roots most deeply. It is from these things that it flowers."

141. "Friendship is the only rose without thorns."

142. "Friends are forever, you might lose them but you'll never forget them."

143. "A ring is round, it has no end, and that is how long I will be your friend."

144. "True friendship multiplies the good in life and divides its evils; strive to have friends, for life without friends is like life on a desert island. To find one real friend in a lifetime is good fortune; to keep him is a blessing."

145. "If you lose at something, a sport for example, a regular friend says 'good try' … but a true friend says 'good try' and helps you to win the next time."

146. "A friend is a shoulder to lean on, an ear to listen, and a heart to comfort."

147. "Keep your friends in your heart and your enemies in your sight."

148. "A good friend is as rare as a left-handed person in a world filled with right-handed people. He simply stands out!"

149. "A friend is like a piece of pie. You never have too many, and they make you happy when you are sad!"

150. "We laughed until we had to cry, we hugged right down to our last goodbye, we were the best we'll ever be, just for a moment, you and me."

151. "Friends stand by each other through thick and thin; every time you need me, I will always be there for you. You make me happy, you make me laugh and you are the best friend anyone can ever have."

152. "When you ask God for a gift, be thankful if He sends out not diamonds, riches, or pearls, but the love of real true friends."

153. "We may laugh, we may cry, but our friendship will never die."

154. "Hold a friend's hand through times of trial. Let her find love through a hug and a smile, but also know when it is time to go — for each and every one of us must learn to grow."

155. "Life is worth all those ups and downs with friends to share them with you!"

156. "A friend is one who knows you as you are, understands where you've been, accepts who you've become, and still invites you to grow."

157. "Friends are super, friends are duper."

158. "True friends, like ivy and the wall, both stand together, and together fall."

159. "The world would be so lonely in sunny hours or gray, without the gift of friendship to help us every day."

160. "On the road between friends' houses, grass does not grow."

161. "Rekindled friendships often burn more brightly."

162. "No matter how strong a friendship may be, it takes years to build the trust and seconds to destroy it."

163. "The best things in life aren't things … they're friends."

164. "Friends are like poems, you may never fully understand them, but you will always love them."

165. "When you're with someone you trust in, never needing to pretend, someone who helps you to know yourself, you know you're with a friend."

166. "Friends are like pillars on your porch. Sometimes they hold you up and sometimes they lean on you."

167. "A friend worth your tears, will never make you cry."

168. "The finest kind of friendship is between two people who expect a great deal of each other, but never ask it."

169. "Friendship is like a garden. It is beautiful when it is watered and tended to with love and care of prayers, hugs,

tears and cheers, but it will be withered up, dry up and die if left untouched."

170. "You lifted me up when I could not lift up myself, you made me smile when I forgot how to, you were there for me in my times of need and you were there for me when I needed nothing at all."

171. "Real friends are those who - when you feel you've made a fool of yourself, don't feel you've done a permanent job."

172. "Having someone who understands is a great blessing for ourselves. Being someone who understands is a great blessing to others."

173. "Friends are like quilts ... give comfort when needed. My sister sent me one. Fate made us sisters ... and love made us friends."

174. "Material things can't make the soul whole. Only the love, trust, and loyalty of friends can do that."

175. "A friend is like a rainbow. They brighten your life when you've been through a storm."

176. "Live every day like it's your last because someday you'll be right!"

177. "A reassuring presence, a light when times are dark, a hand reaching out, is what friendship is about."

178. "Friendship is like a violin ... the cords may loosen time and again, but the melody plays forever."

179. "Friendships multiply joys and divide griefs."

180. "Friends are like walls. Sometimes you lean on them and sometimes it is just enough to know they're there."

181. "Friends are like peanut butter and jelly. They always stick together."

182. "A person is only complete when she has true friends to understand her, share all her passions and sorrows with, and to stand by her throughout life."

183. "A friend is like sunlight, filtering into the quiet corners of one's heart, offering bright new mornings and fresh hope, yet demanding nothing in return."

184. "The greatest challenge in being a friend is not listening when words are spoken, but hearing and feeling even though there is nothing but silence."

185. "The happiest person has three things - a best friend, a true love and a best friend who is their true love."

186. "As love fills through the heart, friendship sees through the eyes."

187. "Don't know what I'd ever do without you from the beginning to the end; you've always been here right beside me so I call you my best friend, through the good times and the bad, whenever I lose or if I win. I know one thing that never changes and that's you as my best friend."

188. "The bird - a nest, the spider - the web, the person - friendship."

189. "An ordinary friend would try to mend your heart once it's been wounded and poured out. A true friend would try to refill it as well."

190. "True friends not only protect you from others when something goes bad, but from yourself when you try to take blame."

191. "A true friend wants nothing more from you than the pleasure of your company."

192. "True friendship is a gift that is given without the expectation of anything in return. Instead, the reward is the friendship itself."

193. "Some people make the world special just by being in it."

194. "The best thing to do behind a person's back is to pat it."

195. "Shared joy is double joy, shared sorrow is half sorrow."

196. "Forget me not, forget me never, and you'll have a friend forever!"

197. "Friends are like chocolate - they are sweet and wonderful, and like its calories, they stick with you."

198. "Through good times and bad times, true friends are always there by your side and when you're in need of caring and need a shoulder to cry on."

199. "A friend is someone that has the courage to tell you that you are wrong."

200. "Friendship is the hardest thing in the world to explain. It's not something you can be taught in school, but if you

haven't learned the value of friendship, you haven't really learned anything at all."

201. "A friend is like a seatbelt - you may not always need them, but they will be there just in case!"

202. "You can pick your friends and you can pick your nose, but you can't pick your friend's nose."

203. "When you cherish the value of a gift of friendship, it can never be lost, for what you always carry in your heart is yours to keep forever and your friends too."

204. "I value the friend who finds time for me in their calendar, I cherish the friend who does not consult her calendar."

205. "A true friend thinks of you when all others are thinking of themselves."

206. "You can make more friends in two months by becoming interested in people, than you can in two years by trying to get people interested in you."

207. "Friendship is the poetry of life."

208. "If you are attracted to the right kind of friends, when you start to go wrong, they will keep you going right."

209. "A song is a moment, a friend is a time, a best friend is a lifetime."

210. "Don't judge yourself by your friends, judge yourself by your best friend."

211. "A best friend is like a four-leaf clover - hard to find, but lucky to have."

212. "Don't make excuses - your enemies won't believe them and your friends don't need to hear them.

213. "We don't have to change friends, if we understand that friends change."

214. "Near each other or miles apart, good friends are always close to the heart."

215. "A friend is someone whom we can always count on to count on us."

216. "A friend multiplies joys and divides sorrows."

217. "If you have one true friend in your lifetime, you are lucky."

218. "Amuse your friends and annoy your enemies."

219. "A friend is one who knows what you're thinking without even saying a word."

220. "Let's become little old ladies together - we'll stay up late looking at old pictures, telling 'remember when' stories, and laughing till our sides ache. Let's become eccentric together - the kind of old ladies who take long walks, wear silly hats, and get away with acting outrageous in public places. And if anybody should ask how long we've been friends, we'll say, 'Oh, forever - since before you were even born!' Let's become little old ladies together - because a friendship that's as special as ours can only grow better through the years."

221. "Friendships come and go, like waves upon the sand, like day and night, like birds in flight, like snowflakes when

they land, but you and I are something else, our friendship's here to say, like weeds and rocks and old dirty socks - it never goes away!"

222. "A true friend will go to hell for you. An enemy will certainly try to send you there."

223. "The trick is not to die for a friend, but to find a friend worth dying for."

224. "Nothing in high school is important enough to affect anyone's life beyond college admissions besides your true friends."

225. "If I could give you one gift my friend, I would give you the ability to see yourself as others do, so you would know how very special you are."

226. "If I had never met you, I wouldn't like you. If I didn't like you, I wouldn't love you. If I didn't love you, I wouldn't miss you. But I did, I do and I will."

227. "If out of time, I could pick one moment and keep it shining, always new, of all the days that I have lived, I'd pick the moment I met you."

228. "Friends are the part of our family we get to choose."

229. "A true friend is someone who thinks that you are a good egg even though he knows that you are slightly cracked."

230. "I'll remember the things I did for awhile, but I'll remember the person I did them with forever."

231. "The joy of friendship is not the outstretched hand, nor the kindly smile, nor the joy of companionship. It is the

spiritual inspiration that comes to one when he discovers that someone else believes in him and is willing to trust him."

232. "The best gift in life is knowing that we have someone who loves us unconditionally, who can make us laugh, who is there to listen and who warms our heart. The best gift in life is a best friend."

233. "Friends are notes to life's great songs, a melody that carries you along."

234. "A true friend is there to make you laugh even when you feel like crying."

235. "A real friend is when you can sit alone together and never say a word … and walk away feeling that you have had the best conversation."

236. "A smile makes richer the one who receives it without making poorer the one who gives it."

237. "To the world you may be one person, but to one person, you may be the world."

238. "To have a good friend is one of the highest delights of life, to be a good friend is one of the noblest and most difficult undertakings."

239. "Happiness comes from the ones I love, but its strength that comes from the ones who love me."

240. "A true friend never gets in your way unless you happen to be going down."

241. "Be yourself because the people that mind don't matter and the people that matter don't mind."

242. "Live like today is your last day, love like you've never been hurt, and dance like no one's watching."

243. "We've shared so much laughter, so many tears. We're a spiritual bond that grows stronger each year. We're not sisters by birth, but we knew from the start, something put us together to be sisters by heart."

244. "Friends are the chocolate chips in the cookie of life!"

245. "Friendship is the perfect gift; everyone needs it and no one cares if it is given back."

246. "A hug is the perfect gift; one size fits all; everyone likes them and no one cares if it is given back."

247. "I thank you for all the goodness, kindness, honesty and warmth of feeling that the continuance of our friendship brings."

248. "A friend will ride in the limo with you, but a real friend will ride the bus with you when the limo breaks down."

249. "True friendship multiplies the good in life and divides its evils. Strive to have friends, for life without friends is like life on a desert island. To fine one real friend in a lifetime is good fortune; to keep him is a blessing."

250. "Real friendship is the sharing of all that the heart holds inside, it's tears and laughter, it's joy and broken dreams. Because friendship dwells in the heart where time and distance know boundaries, it understands the depth of true

feelings and the sound of words spoken. It is a true gift, for it connects the heart of soulmates together forever."

251. "Friends are the flowers in the garden of life."

252. "True friendship is like sound health; the value of it is seldom known until it is lost."

253. "A real friend is one who walks in when the rest of the world walks out."

254. "A friend is someone who is there for you when he'd rather be anywhere else."

255. "A friend is one who believes in you when you have ceased to believe in yourself."

256. "A hug is worth a thousand words. A friend is worth more."

257. "Everyone is a friend, until they prove otherwise."

258. "Your friend is the person who knows all about you, and still likes you."

259. "Two may walk together under the same roof for many years, yet never really meet, and two others at first speech are old friends."

260. "Friends are the most important ingredient in this recipe of life."

261. "Strangers are just friends waiting to happen."

262. "Sometimes you pick your friends, sometimes they pick you."

263. "The greatest good you can do for another is not just share your riches, but to reveal to him, his own."

264. "Friends are the Bacon Bits in the salad bowl of life."

265. "It's the friends you can call up at 4 a.m. that matter."

266. "Anybody can sympathize with the sufferings of a friend, but it requires a very fine nature to sympathize with a friend's success."

267. "Grief can take care of itself, but to get the full value of joy you must have somebody to share it with."

268. "A best friend is the one who brings out the best in you."

269. "Friendship without self interest is one of the rare and beautiful things in life."

270. "Best friends are like diamonds, precious and rare. False friends are like leaves, found everywhere."

271. "A good friend is hard to find, hard to lose, and impossible to forget."

272. "When the silences are no longer awkward, you know you are around friends."

273. "The secret to friendship is being a good listener."

274. "A true friend is someone you can trust with all your secrets."

275. "Gems may be precious, but friends are priceless."

276. "Everyone hears what you say. Friends listen to what you say. Best friends listen to what you don't say."

277. "Material things can't make the soul whole. Only the love, trust, and loyalty of friends can do that."

278. "Money might make you wealthy, but friends make you rich."

279. "A friend loves you, makes you feel alright, troubles are not troubles when you talk, listen and accept you as you are, because you will feel the same and love the same ..."

280. "Friendship is what gets you through the bad times and helps you enjoy the good times."

281. "Having someone who understands is a great blessing for ourselves. Being someone who understands is a great blessing to others."

282. "Any day is sunny that's brightened by a smile ... Any friendship blossoms if it's tended to with style."

283. "The better you know someone, the less there is to say. Or maybe, there's less that needs to be said."

284. "Every gift from a friend is a wish for your happiness."

285. "The most beautiful discovery that true friends can make is that they can grow separately without growing apart."

286. "You only meet your once in a lifetime friend ... once in a lifetime."

287. "A friend will be there for you when things are good ... but a TRUE friend will be there for you when things are good and also when things are very bad ... and just when it feels like you will never smile again, she can put a smile on your face with just a hug!"

288. "A friend will strengthen you with her prayers, bless you with her love, and encourage you with her hope."

289. "I'd like to be the sort of friend that you have been to me. I'd like to be the help you've always been glad to be; I'd

like to mean as much to you each minute of the day, as you have meant, old friend of mine, to me along the way."

290. "A friend is like a rainbow. They brighten your life when you've been through a storm."

291. "A reassuring presence, a light when times are dark, a hand reaching out, is what friendship is about."

292. "Friendship is like a popsicle on two sticks, when the friendship breaks, so does the popsicle, making everything a mess."

293. "Love doesn't make the world go round, it makes the ride worthwhile."

294. "A friend you have to buy, won't be worth what you pay for him."

295. "With clothes the new are the best, with friends the old are the best.":

296. "Friendship is like thighs, they are always sticking together."

297. "True friends are never apart, maybe in distance, but not in heart."

298. "A real friend will tell you when you have spinach stuck in your teeth."

299. "Shared sorrow is half sorrow, shared joy is double joy."

300. "Most people come into our lives and quickly leave. It is the special few that come in and leave a footprint in our hearts, and we are forever changed."

301. "Remember that every good friend was once a stranger."

USEFUL QUOTATIONS

1. "Heaven is where the police are British, the cooks are French, the mechanics German, the lovers Italian and it's all organized by the Swiss. Hell is where the chefs are British, the mechanics French, the lovers Swiss, the police German, and it's all organized by the Italians."

2. "The trouble with being punctual is that nobody's there to appreciate it."

3. "I think animal testing is a terrible idea; they get all nervous and give the wrong answers."

4. "The hypothalamus is one of the most important parts of the brain, involved in many kinds of motivation, among other functions. The hypothalamus controls the 'Four F's': 1. fighting; 2. fleeing; 3. feeding; and 4. mating.

5. "I am not a vegetarian because I love animals; I am a vegetarian because I hate plants."

6. "There's an old story about the person who wished his computer were as easy to use as his telephone. That wish has come true, since I no longer know how to use my telephone."

7. "Experience is the marvelous thing that enables you to recognize a mistake when you make it again."

8. "My opinions may have changed, but not the fact that I am right."

9. "Her kisses left something to be desired — the rest of her."

10. "You know what would make a good story? Something about a clown who makes people happy, but inside he's real sad. Also, he has severe diarrhea."

11. "If a kid asks where rain comes from, I think a cute thing to tell him is 'God is crying.' And if he asks why God is crying, another cute thing to tell him is probably because of something you did."

12. "One thing kids like is to be tricked. For instance, I was going to take my little nephew to Disneyland, but instead I drove him to an old burned-out warehouse. 'Oh no,' I said, 'Disneyland burned down.' He cried and cried, but I think deep down he thought it was a pretty good joke. I started to drive over to the real Disneyland, but it was getting pretty late."

13. "When I was a kid, my favorite relative was Uncle Caveman. After school, we'd all go play in his cave, and every once in awhile, he would eat one of us. It wasn't until later that I found out that Uncle Caveman was a bear."

14. "In weightlifting, I don't think sudden, uncontrolled urination should automatically disqualify you."

15. "Sure God created man before woman. But then, you always make a rough draft before the final masterpiece."

16. "Marriage is the triumph of imagination over intelligence. Second marriage is the triumph of hope over experience."

17. "The secret of success is sincerity. Once you can fake that, you've got it made."

18. "An intellectual snob is someone who can listen to the William Tell Overture and not think of the Lone Ranger."

19. "Why is it that our memory is good enough to retain the least triviality that happens to us, and yet not good enough to recollect how often we have told it to the same person!"

20. "It matters not whether you win or lose; what matters is whether I win or lose."

21. "Health is merely the slowest possible rate at which one can die."

22. "The optimist proclaims that we live in the best of all possible worlds; and the pessimist fears this is true."

23. "He who hesitates is not only lost, but miles from the next exit."

24. "Don't think of it as being outnumbered, think of it as a wide target selection."

25. "There are two essential basic strategies for success in business: 1. never reveal all you know."

26. "Analyzing humor is like dissecting a frog; nobody enjoys it, and the frog usually dies as a result."

27. "A youth becomes a man when the marks he wants to leave on the world have nothing to do with tires."

28. "Talk is cheap because supply exceeds demand."

29. "Don't cry because it's over, smile because it happened."

30. "I'm sorry, you seem to have mistaken me for someone who cares."

31. "We the unwilling working for the ungrateful are doing the impossible. We have done so much, for so long, with so little, we are now qualified to do anything with nothing."

32. "You don't have to agree with me, but it's quicker."

33. "You spend your whole life believing that you're on the right track, only to discover that you're on the wrong train."

34. "Maturity is knowing when and where to be immature."

35. "The world is full of apathy, but nobody seems to care."

36. "Where there is a will, there is an inheritance tax."

37. "Change is inevitable, except from vending machines."

38. "If you had your left arm cut off, your right arm would be left."

39. "Never be afraid to try something new. Remember, amateurs built the ark, professionals built the Titanic."

MURPHY'S LAWS

1. "If anything can go wrong, it will."

2. "If there is a possibility of several things going wrong, the one that will cause the most damage will be the one to go wrong."

3. "Corollary: If there is a worse time for something to go wrong, it will happen then."

4. "If anything just cannot go wrong, it will anyway."

5. "If you perceive that there are four possible ways in which something can go wrong, and circumvent these, then a fifth way, unprepared for, will promptly develop."

6. "Left to themselves, things tend to go from bad to worse."

7. "If everything seems to be going well, you have obviously overlooked something."

8. "Nature always sides with the hidden flaw."

9. "Nothing is as easy as it looks."

10. "Everything takes longer than you think."

11. "Whenever you set out to do something, something else must be done first."

12. "Every solution breeds new problems."

13. "The legibility of a copy is inversely proportional to its importance."

14. "Matter will be damaged in direct proportion to its value."

15. "A falling object will always land where it can do the most damage."

16. "A shatterproof object will always fall on the only surface hard enough to crack or break it."

17. "The chance of the bread falling with the buttered side down is directly proportional to the cost of the carpet."

18. "You will always find something in the last place you look."

19. "After you bought a replacement for something you've lost and searched for everywhere, you'll find the original."

20. "No matter how long or how hard you shop for an item, after you've bought it, it will be on sale somewhere cheaper."

21. "The other line always moves faster."

22. "Build a system that even a fool can use, and only a fool will use it."

23. "Everyone has a scheme for getting rich that will not work."

24. "In any hierarchy, each individual rises to his own level of incompetence, and then remains there."

25. "There's never time to do it right, but there's always time to do it over."

26. "When in doubt, mumble. When in trouble, delegate."

27. "Anything good in life is either illegal, immoral or fattening."

28. "Murphy's golden rule: whoever has the gold makes the rules."

29. "A Smith & Wesson beats four aces."

30. "In case of doubt, make it sound convincing."

31. "Never argue with a fool. People might not know the difference."

32. "Whatever hits the fan will not be evenly distributed."

33. "No good deed goes unpunished."

34. "Where patience fails, force prevails."

35. "Anything dropped in the bathroom will fall in the toilet."

36. "If you want something bad enough, chances are you won't get it."

37. "If you think you are doing the right thing, chances are it will backfire in your face."

38. "When waiting for traffic, chances are that when one lane clears, the other is congested."

39. "Just when you think things cannot get any worse, they will."

40. "Remember the "Boomer rang" effect; whatever you do will always come back."

41. "If you re-act to actions, you've acted on actions."

42. "He who angers you controls you, therefore you have no control over your anger."

43. "Any time you put an item in a 'safe place', it will never be seen again."

44. "Your best golf shots always occur when playing alone."

45. "The worst golf shots always occur when playing with someone you are trying to impress."

46. "No matter how hard you try, you cannot push a string (getting everyone in the family to the car at the same time, for example)."

47. "The fish are always biting … yesterday!"

48. "The cost of the hairdo is directly related to the strength of the wind."

49. "Great ideas are never remembered and dumb statements are never forgotten."

50. "The clothes washer/dryer will only eat one of each pair of socks."

51. "The light at the end of the tunnel is a train."

52. "Whatever you want, you can't have. What you can have, you don't want."

53. "Whatever you want to do, is not possible. Whatever is possible for you to do, you don't want to do it."

54. "Traffic is inversely proportional to how late you are, or are going to be."

55. "The complexity and frustration factor is inversely proportional to how much time you have left to finish, and how important it is."

56. "If you say something, and stake your reputation on it, you will lose your reputation."

57. "Anything that can go wrong, has already gone wrong! You just haven't been notified."

58. "Ants will always infest the nearest food cupboard."

59. "Those who know the least will always know it the loudest."

60. "Things always go from bad to worse."

61. "A person without values or standards can never be a hypocrite."

62. "A bird in the hand is messy."

63. "When you wear new shoes for the first time, everyone will step on them.

64. "If at first you don't succeed, destroy all evidence that you ever tried."

65. "It takes forever to learn the rules and once you've learned them, they change again."

MURPHY'S COMPUTER LAWS

1. "Any given program, when running, is obsolete."

2. "Any given program costs more and takes longer each time it is run."

3. "If a program is useful, it will have to be changed."

4. "If a program is useless, it will have to be documented."

5. "Any given program will expand to fill all the available memory."

6. "The value of a program is inversely proportional to the weight of its output."

7. "Program complexity grows until it exceeds the capability of the programmer who must maintain it."

8. "Every non-trivial program has at least one bug. Corollary 1: A sufficient condition for program triviality is that it have no bugs. Corollary 2: At least one bug will be observed after the author leaves the organization."

9. "Bugs will appear in one part of a working program when another 'unrelated' part is modified."

10. "The subtlest bugs cause the greatest damage and problems. Corollary: A subtle bug will modify storage, thereby masquerading as some other problem."

11. "A 'debugged' program that crashes will wipe out source files on storage devices when there is the least available backup."

12. "A hardware failure will cause system software to crash, and the customer engineer will blame the programmer."

13. "A system software crash will cause hardware to act strangely and the programmers will blame the customer engineer."

14. "Undetectable errors are infinite in variety, in contrast to detectable errors, which by definition are limited."

15. "Adding manpower to a late software project makes it later."

16. "Make it possible for programmers to write programs in English, and you will find that programmers cannot write in English."

17. "The documented interfaces between standard software modules will have undocumented quirks."

18. "The probability of a hardware failure disappearing is inversely proportional to the distance between the computer and the customer engineer."

19. "A working program is one that has only unobserved bugs."

20. "No matter how many resources you have, it is never enough."

21. "Any cool program always requires more memory than you have."

22. "When you finally buy enough memory, you will not have enough disk space."

23. "Disks are always full. It is futile to try to get more disk space. Data expands to fill any void."

24. "If a program actually fits in memory and has enough disk space, it is guaranteed to crash."

25. "If such a program has not crashed yet, it is waiting for a critical moment before it crashes."

26. "No matter how good of a deal you get on computer components, the price will always drop immediately after the purchase."

27. "All components become obsolete."

28. "The speed with which components become obsolete is directly proportional to the price of the component."

29. "Software bugs are impossible to detect by anybody except the end user."

30. "The maintenance engineer will never have seen a model quite like yours before."

31. "It is axiomatic that any spares required will have just been discontinued and will be no longer in stock."

32. "Any manufacturer making his warranties dependent upon the device being earthed will only supply power cabling with two wires."

33. "If a circuit requires 'n' components, then there will be only 'n-1' components in locally- held stocks."

34. "A failure in a device will never appear until it has passed final inspection.

35. "A program generator creates programs that are more buggy than the program generator."

36. "All constants are variables."

37. "A part dropped from the workbench will roll to a degree of un-reachability proportional to its importance."

38. "In a transistor circuit protected by a fuse, the transistor will always blow to protect the fuse."

39. "No matter how hard you work, the boss will only appear when you access the Internet."

40. "The hard drive on your computer will only crash when it contains vital information that has not been backed up."

41. "Computers don't make errors - what they do, they do on purpose."

42. "Each computer code has five bugs, and this number does not depend on how many bugs have been already found (it is conservative)."

43. "Profanity is one language all computer users know."

44. "The number of bugs always exceeds the number of lines found in a program."

45. "The most ominous words for those using computers: 'Daddy, what does now formatting Drive C mean?'"

46. "When putting something into memory, always remember where you put it."

47. "Every non-trivial program can be simplified to one line of code, and it will contain a bug."

48. "An expert is someone brought in at the last minute to share the blame."

49. "Debugging is at least twice as hard as writing the program in the first place. So if your code is as clever as you can possibly make it, then by definition, you're not smart enough to debug it."

50. "For any given software, the moment you manage to master it, a new version appears."

51. "The new versions always manages to change the one feature you need most."

MURPHY'S TECHNOLOGY LAWS

1. "Logic is a systematic method of coming to the wrong conclusion with confidence."

2. "Whenever a system becomes completely defined, some fool discovers something which either abolishes the system or expands it beyond recognition."

3. "Technology is dominated by those who manage what they do not understand."

4. "If builders built buildings the way programmers wrote programs, then the first woodpecker that came along would destroy civilization."

5. "The opulence of the front office decor varies inversely with the fundamental solvency of the firm."

6. "The attention span of a computer is only as long as its electrical cord."

7. "An expert is one who knows more and more about less and less, until he knows absolutely everything about nothing."

8. "Tell a man there are 300 billion stars in the universe and he'll believe you. Tell him a bench has wet paint on it and he'll have to touch to be sure."

9. "All great discoveries are made by mistake."

10. "Always draw your curves, then plot your reading."

11. "Nothing ever gets built on schedule or within budget."

12. "All's well that ends."

13. "A meeting is an event at which the minutes are kept and the hours are lost."

14. "The first myth of management is that it exists."

15. "New systems generate new problems."

16. "To err is human, but to really foul things up requires a computer."

17. "We don't know one millionth of one percent about anything."

18. "Any sufficiently advanced technology is indistinguishable."

19. "A computer makes as many mistakes in two seconds as 20 men working 20 years make."

20. "Nothing motivates a man more than to see his boss putting in an honest day's work."

21. "Some people manage by the book, even though they don't know who wrote the book or even what book."

22. "The primary function of the design engineer is to make things difficult for the fabricator and impossible for the serviceman."

23. "To spot the expert, pick the one who predicts the job will take the longest and cost the most."

24. "After all is said and done, a hell of a lot more is said than done."

25. "Any circuit design must contain at least one part which is obsolete, two parts which are unobtainable and three parts which are still under development."

26. "A complex system that works is invariably found to have evolved from a simple system that works."

27. "If mathematically you end up with the incorrect answer, try multiplying by the page number."

28. "Computers are unreliable, but humans are even more unreliable. Any system which depends on human reliability is unreliable."

29. "Give all orders verbally. Never write anything down that might go into a 'Pearl Harbor File.'"

30. "Under the most rigorously controlled conditions of pressure, temperature, volume, humidity, and other variables, the organism will do as it damn well pleases."

31. "If you can't understand it, it is intuitively obvious."

32. "The more cordial the buyer's secretary, the greater the odds that the competition already has the order."

33. "In designing any type of construction, no overall dimension can be totaled correctly after 4:30 P.M. on Friday. The correct total will become self-evident at 8:15 a.m. on Monday."

34. "Fill what's empty. Empty what's full. And scratch where it itches."

35. "All things are possible except skiing through a revolving door."

36. "The only perfect science is hind-sight."

37. "Work smarter and not harder and be careful of yor speling."

38. "If it's not in the computer, it doesn't exist."

39. "If an experiment works, something has gone wrong."

40. "When all else fails, read the instructions,"

41. "If there is a possibility of several things going wrong, the one that will cause the most damage will be the one to go wrong."

42. "Everything that goes up, must come down, maybe."

43. "Any instrument when dropped will roll into the least accessible corner."

44. "Any simple theory will be worded in the most complicated way."

45. "The degree of technical competence is inversely proportional to the level of management."

46. "A difficult task will be halted near completion by one tiny, previously insignificant detail."

47. "There is never time to do it right, but always time to do it over."

48. "The remaining work to finish in order to reach your goal increases as the deadline approaches."

49. "If there is ever the possibility of several things to go wrong, the one that will cause the most damage will be the one to go wrong."

50. "If something breaks, and it stops you from doing something, it will be fixed when you: a. no longer need it; b. are in the middle of something else; c. don't want it to

be fixed, because you really don't want to do what you were supposed to do."

51. "Each profession talks to itself in its own language, apparently there is no Rosetta Stone."

52. "The more urgent the need for a decision to be made, less apparent becomes the identity of the decision maker."

53. "It is never wise to let a piece of electronic equipment know that you are in a hurry."

54. "Don't fix something that ain't broke, 'cause you'll break it and you still can't fix it."

55. "You can never tell which way the train went by looking at the track."

56. "If you are not thoroughly confused, you have not been thoroughly informed."

57. "A screw will never fit a nut."

58. "Standard parts are not."

59. "When working on a motor vehicle engine, any tool dropped will land directly under the center of the engine."

60. "Interchangeable tapes won't."

61. "Never trust modern technology. Trust it only when it is old technology."

62. "The bolt that is in the most awkward place will always be the one with the tightest thread."

63. "The most ominous phase in science: "_Uh_-oh ...""

64. "Any example of hardware/software can be made fool-proof. It cannot, however, be made damn-fool-proof."

65. "In today's fast-moving tech environment, it is a requirement that we forget more than we learn."

MURPHY'S LOVE LAWS

1. "All the good ones are taken. If the person isn't taken, there's a reason."

2. "The nicer someone is, the farther away (s)he is from you."

3. "Brains x Beauty x Availability = Constant. The constant is always zero."

4. "The amount of love someone feels for you is inversely proportional to how much you love them."

5. "Money can't buy love, but it sure gets you a great bargaining position."

6. "The best things in the world are free — and worth every penny of it."

7. "Every kind action has a not-so-kind reaction."

8. "Nice guys (girls) finish last."

9. "If it seems too good to be true, it probably is."

10. "Availability is a function of time. The minute you get interested is the minute they find someone else."

11. "The more beautiful the woman is who loves you, the easier it is to leave her with no hard feelings."

12. "Nothing improves with age."

13. "No matter how many times you've had it, if it's offered, take it, because it'll never be quite the same again."

14. "Virginity can be cured."

15. "When a man's wife learns to understand him, she usually stops listening to him."

16. "The qualities that most attract a woman to a man are usually the same ones she can't stand years later."

17. "Sex is dirty only if it's done right."

18. "The best way to hold a man is in your arms."

19. "When the lights are out, all women are beautiful."

20. "Sex is hereditary. If your parents never had it, chances are you won't either."

21. "Sow your wild oats on Saturday night — then on Sunday pray for crop failure."

22. "The game of love is never called off on account of darkness."

23. "It was not the apple on the tree but the pair on the ground that caused the trouble in the garden."

24. "Sex discriminates against the shy and the ugly."

25. "Before you find your handsome prince, you've got to kiss a lot of frogs."

26. "There may be some things better than sex, and some things worse than sex. But there is nothing exactly like it."

27. "Love your neighbor, but don't get caught."

28. "If the effort that went in research on the female bosom had gone into our space program, we would now be running hot-dog stands on the moon."

29. "Love is a matter of chemistry, sex is a matter of physics."

30. "Sex is a three-letter word which needs some old-fashioned four-letter words to convey its full meaning."

31. "One good turn gets most of the blankets."

32. "You cannot produce a baby in one month by impregnating nine women."

33. "Love is the triumph of imagination over intelligence."

34. "It is better to have loved and lost than never to have loved at all."

35. "Abstain from wine, women, and song; mostly song."

36. "Never argue with a women when she's tired — or rested."

37. "A woman never forgets the men she could have had; a man, the women he couldn't."

38. "It is better to be looked over than overlooked."

39. "Folks playing leapfrog must complete all jumps."

40. "Beauty is skin deep; ugly goes right to the bone."

41. "Never stand between a fire hydrant and a dog."

42. "A man is only a man, but a good bicycle is a ride."

43. "Love comes in spurts."

44. "Sex is one of the nine reasons for reincarnation; the other eight are unimportant."

45. "Smile, it makes people wonder what you are thinking."

46. "There is no difference between a wise man and a fool when they fall in love."

47. "Never go to bed mad, stay up and fight."

48. "Nothing improves with age."

49. "When a man wants his wife to hear, she doesn't listen. When that same man doesn't want his wife to hear, she's all ears."

50. "Love and high-school must NEVER go together."

51. "If a man speaks deep in the forest and there is no woman there to hear him, is he still wrong?"

52. "No one is as fascinating as they think."

53. "If you believe a relationship can't work, but feel the need to try, it won't. Corollary: You will later find out that your lack of belief caused it to fail."

54. "The duration of a relationship to a person is inversely proportionate to the importance of person to you."

55. "The key to a woman's heart is an unexpected gift at an unexpected time."

56. "Love makes believers of us all. Translation: Love obscures common sense."

57. "Being taken attracts women. Being single makes them avoid you like the plague."

58. "Celibacy is not heredity."

59. "Horniness is inversely related to one's chance of scoring."

60. "The man shalt not win the argument he started."

61. "The man shalt not win the argument he didn't start."

62. "If a man won an argument, it was just in his head."

63. "A love will tell you they love you endlessly. A true love will tell everyone else they love you endlessly."

64. "When all else fails, have hope."

65. "In romance; and in finance we play with figures."

66. "Sex on the TV can't hurt you unless you fall off."

67. "Anticipation is 98% of the pleasure."

68. "The amount of members of the opposite sex you pursue is inversely proportional to pretty much everything about you, such as intelligence."

MURPHY'S REAL ESTATE INVESTOR LAWS

1. "That sweet little girl with the baby that you rented to, will start dating the mad motorcycle man from hell ... and several of his friends ... the very next week."

2. "Tenants have at least one relative get sick or die per month, so ... they will just have to pay you later."

3. "If a tenant attempts to replace the washer in a faucet, plan on replacing the faucet; perhaps all the plumbing in the building."

4. "Prospective tenants who make an appointment to see your rental across town, often get kidnapped on the way there ... so there was just no way they could call you."

5. "Tenants only lock themselves out in the middle of the night ... or on Christmas."

6. "When a furnace breaks in mid-winter, it is always the heat exchanger."

7. "At least one tenant's check will be "lost in the mail" every month."

8. "Every lost pet will find its way to your rental."

9. "The hardware store closes five minutes before you get there."

10. "A tenant's ability to see dirt and damage is much greater when they move in than when they move out."

11. "Your best tenants always get job transfers during the worst rental markets."

12. "Everything in your rentals will break 100 times faster than in your own home."

13. "The insurance inspector always shows up to take photos of the building as you are putting the evicted tenant's possessions on the curb."

14. "Tenants always swear under oath that the window was broken when they moved in."

15. "When a tenant calls and says, 'Hi, how are you?' something is drastically wrong."

16. "If it exists, your tenant will try to flush it down the toilet."

17. "If you have any questions about anything, ask your tenants."

18. "If it is pouring rain, you can be sure the windows are open at one or more of your units."

19. "Proper disposal of chewing gum is in the carpet."

20. "All cracks in tile are due to the settling of the structure, never by a dropped object."

MURPHY'S TEACHING & STUDENT LAWS

1. "The clock in the instructor's room will be wrong."

2. "Disaster will occur when visitors are in the room."

3. "A subject interesting to the teacher will bore students."

4. "The time a teacher takes in explaining is inversely proportional to the information retained by students."

5. "A meeting's length will be directly proportional to the boredom the speaker produces."

6. "Students who are doing better are credited with working harder. If children start to do poorly, the teacher will be blamed."

7. "The problem child will be a school board member's son."

8. "When the instructor is late, he will meet the principal in the hall."

9. "If the instructor is late and does not meet the principal, the instructor is late to the faculty meeting."

10. "New students come from schools that do not teach anything."

11. "Good students move away."

12. "When speaking to the school psychologist, the teacher will say: 'weirdo' rather than 'emotionally disturbed.'"

13. "The school board will make a better pay offer before the teacher's union negotiates."

14. "The instructor's study hall will be the largest in several years."

Roasts and Toasts Made Easy

15. "The administration will view the study hall as the teacher's preparation time."

16. "Clocks will run more quickly during free time."

17. "On a test day, at least 15% of the class will be absent."

18. "If the instructor teaches art, the principal will be an ex-coach and will dislike art. If the instructor is a coach, the principal will be an ex-coach who took a winning team to the state finals."

19. "There are no answers in libraries, only cross references."

20. "If the course you wanted most has room for "n" students, you will be the "n+1" to apply."

21. "Class schedules are designed so that every student will waste maximum time between classes. Corollary: When you are occasionally able to schedule two classes in a row, they will be held in classrooms at opposite ends of the campus."

22. "A prerequisite for a desired course will be offered only during the semester following the desired course."

23. "When reviewing your notes before an exam, the most important ones will be illegible."

24. "The more studying you did for the exam, the less sure you are as to which answer they want."

25. "Eighty percent of the final exam will be based on the one lecture you missed about the one book you didn't read."

26. "The night before the English history midterm, your Biology instructor will assign two hundred pages on

127

planarian. Corollary: Every instructor assumes that you have nothing else to do except study for that instructor's course."

27. "If you are given an open-book exam, you will forget your book. Corollary: If you are given a take home exam, you will forget where you live."

28. "At the end of the semester you will recall having enrolled in a course at the beginning of the semester—and never attending."

29. "Pocket calculator batteries that have lasted all semester will fail during the math final. Corollary: If you bring extra batteries, they will be defective."

30. "In your toughest final, the most distractingly attractive student in class will sit next to you for the first time."

31. "Anything in parentheses can be ignored."

32. "You never catch on until after the test."

33. "The one course you must take to graduate will not be offered during your last semester."

34. "The book or periodical most vital to the completion of your term paper will be missing from the library. Corollary: If it is available, the most important page will be torn out."

35. "The most valuable quotation will be the one for which you cannot determine the course. Corollary: The source for an un-attributed quotation will appear in the most hostile review of your work."

36. "The more general the title of a course, the less you will learn from it."

37. "The more specific a title is, the less you will be able to apply it later."

38. "The closest library doesn't have the material you need."

39. "No matter which book you need, it's on the bottom shelf."

40. "When a student asks for a second time if you have read his book report, he did not read the book."

41. "If attendance is mandatory, a scheduled exam will produce increased absenteeism. If attendance is optional, an exam will produce persons you have never seen before."

42. "You can't misspell numbers when you write them as digits."

43. "The back of the room is never far enough."

MURPHY'S LAWS OF COMMERCE

1. "The first 90% of a project takes 90% of the time, the last 10% takes the other 90% of the time."

2. "If you can't get your work done in the first 24 hours, work nights."

3. "A pat on the back is only a few inches from a kick in the pants."

4. "Don't be irreplaceable, if you can't be replaced, you can't be promoted."

5. "It doesn't matter what you do, it only matters what you say you've done and what you say you're going to do."

6. "After any salary raise, you will have less money at the end of the month than you did before."

7. "The more crap you put up with, the more crap you are going to get."

8. "You can go anywhere you want if you look serious and carry a clipboard."

9. "Eat one live toad first thing in the morning and nothing worse will happen to you the rest of the day."

10. "Never ask two questions in a business letter. The reply will discuss the one you are least interested in, and say nothing about the other."

11. "When the bosses talk about improving productivity, they are never talking about themselves."

12. "If at first you don't succeed, try again. Then quit. No use being a fool about it."

13. "There will always be beer cans rolling on the floor of your car when the boss asks for a ride home from the office."

14. "The boss is always right."

15. "Mother said there would be days like this, but she never said there would be so many."

16. "Keep your boss's boss off your boss's back."

17. "Everything can be filed under 'miscellaneous.'"

18. "Never delay the ending of a meeting or the beginning of a cocktail hour."

19. "To err is human, to forgive is not company policy."

20. "In case of an atomic bomb attack, work rules will be temporarily suspended."

21. "Anyone can do any amount of work provided it isn't the work he is supposed to be doing."

22. "Important letters that contain no errors will develop errors in the mail."

23. "The last person that quit or was fired will be the one held responsible for everything that goes wrong - until the next person quits or is fired."

24. "There is never enough time to do it right the first time, but there is always enough time to do it over."

25. "The more pretentious a corporate name, the smaller the organization."

26. "If you are good, you will be assigned all the work. If you are really good, you will get out of it."

27. "You are always doing something marginal when the boss drops by your desk."

28. "If someone says he will do something 'without fail', he won't."

29. "People who go to conferences are the ones who shouldn't."

30. "People are always available for work in the past tense."

31. "People don't make the same mistake twice, they make it three, four, or five times."

32. "If it wasn't for the last minute, nothing would get done."

33. "At work, the authority of a person is inversely proportional to the number of pens that person is carrying."

34. "When you don't know what to do, walk fast and look worried."

35. "You will always get the greatest recognition for the job you least like."

36. "No one gets sick on Wednesdays."

37. "Getting the job done is no excuse for not following the rules."

38. "Following the rules will not get the job done."

39. "When confronted by a difficult problem, you can solve it more easily by reducing it to the question, 'How would the Lone Ranger handle this?'"

40. "No matter how much you do, you never do enough."

41. "The longer the title, the less important the job."

42. "Machines that have broken down will work perfectly when the repairman arrives."

43. "Progress is only made on alternate Tuesdays."

44. "An 'acceptable' level of employment means that the government economist to whom it is acceptable still has a job."

45. "Once a job is fouled up, anything done to improve it only makes it worse."

46. "The employee who has performed his duties faithfully and without fault for 5 years will be given an increase of five cents per day in his pay - provided the profits allow it."

47. "All vacations and holidays create problems, except for one's own."

48. "Success is a matter of luck, just ask any failure."

49. "The value of any job task is inversely proportional to its deadline."

50. "When you see an item in the flyer, by the time you get to the store, it's either sold out or the price has doubled."

51. "The person at the meeting or discussion who is right will be the person who has not listened and will later be blamed for coming up with the bad idea."

52. "Just when you have no cash, you are in great pain and got to the bank to find the bank computers offline."

53. "Bills travel through the mail twice as fast as checks."

54. "No man is an island, until it comes to paying the bills."

55. "If you have a little extra money to blow, something will break, and cost more than that little extra."

56. "If you don't want it, there is plenty of it; if you really need it, they're all out of it. The more you like a product, the more likely it will be discontinued."

57. "If you are shopping to find a certain thing, no matter how simple it may be, no matter where you go, you will find every conceivable thing except that which you are looking for."

58. "The one time you didn't make a copy of your 1040, that's the one the IRS did not receive."

ENDING THE ROAST

The Roast can end on either a humorous note with a closing joke or a more serious one with a closing story or poem that shares your true admiration and respect for the Roastee.

Sample Endings

* Humorous:

    * I've poked a lot of fun at John tonight, but I want you all to know that I didn't use half the stuff I could have used.

    * I've been to many Roasts in my day, but I must say that I've never seen an honoree who was so worthy of everything that was said about him and had so little idea of what was going on.

* Poems:

    The following poems are examples of some that are appropriate for closing the Roast. These were written by Edgar A. Guest, but any bookstore or library has many other references which can be used.

A FRIEND

A friend is one who takes your hand
And talks a speech you understand;
He's partly kindness, partly mirth,
And faith unfaltering in your worth;
He's first to cheer you on success,
And last to leave you in distress;
A friend is constant, honest, true —
In short, old pal, he's just like YOU!

A LOYAL FRIEND

Ain't it good when life seems dreary
And your hopes about to end,
Just to feel the handclasp cheery
Of a fine and loyal friend?
Ain't it fine when things are going
Topsy-turvy and askew,
To discover someone showing
Good old-fashioned faith in you?

LIFE

Life is a gift to be used every day,

Not to be smothered and hidden away;

It isn't a thing to be stored in the chest

Where you gather your keepsakes and treasure your best;

It isn't a joy to be sipped now and then,

And promptly put back in a dark place again.

Life is a gift that the humblest boast of,

And one that the humblest may well make the most of;

Get out and live it each hour of the day,

Wear it and use it as much as you may;

Don't keep it in niches and corners and grooves –

You'll find that in service, its beauty improves.

COMPENSATION

I'd like to think when life is done

That I had filled a needed post,

That here and there I'd paid my fare

With more than idle talk and boast;

That I had taken gifts divine,

The breath of life and manhood fine,

137

And tried to use them now and then
In service for my fellow men.

I'd hate to think when life is through
That I had lived my round of years
A useless kind, that leaves behind
No record in this vale of tears;
That I had wasted all my days
By treading only selfish ways,
And that this world would be the same
If it had never known my name.

I'd like to think that here and there,
When I am gone, there shall remain
A happier spot that might have not
Existed had I toiled for gain;
That someone's cheery voice and smile
Shall prove that I had been worthwhile;
That I had paid with something fine
My debt to God for life divine.

TOASTS

Introduction

A Toast is a great opportunity to have a positive effect on any kind of social or business event. In doing so, you can establish yourself as a person of great wit and you will be eagerly sought after to help enliven these occasions. Usually all that is needed is a glass of any kind containing a liquid of any kind — from water to champagne. However, sometimes any object can be raised and used. For example, at any meal, a piece of bread can be Toasted by saying, "Here's to the baker, a real loafer who makes lots of dough." Or, "Let's Toast this bread since without bread, we would not have toast."

The Toast can be short and impromptu or somewhat longer and planned such as a best man toasting the bride and groom at their wedding. Almost any subject at any occasion is fair game for a well applied and delivered Toast. Properly done at an appropriate time, the Toast can change the direction or atmosphere of a gathering, relieve tensions, and effectively get things going when there is a pause in the conversation.

Toasts have been around for a long time. It is rumored that the first Toast was done by Adam when he said, "Here's to Eve, the only woman in the world for me." Toasts can be original, repeats or take-offs of prior Toasts or quotes from well known people such as the man who was being honored at a dinner and said, "I really don't deserve this, but I have arthritis and I don't deserve that either."

Larry Miller

A nice way to start any meal is the Toast, "Eat, drink and be merry, for tomorrow you diet."

To sum up, almost any time is a good time for a Toast. By anticipating and preparing for these opportunities, they can be made much more enjoyable for all concerned.

Sample Toasts

Although we are all familiar with events where Toasts are commonplace, there are many less obvious areas where a Toast can be fun and effective. Some examples of both are:

<u>Jobs and Professions</u>

   * Farmers: Good luck to the hoof and the horn

                         Good luck to the flock and the fleece

                         Good luck to the growers of corn

                         With an abundance of plenty and peace.

                         Farmers are always outstanding in their fields.

   * Minters: To our minters — they make tons of money without any advertising.

   * Dentists: Whose living depends on working from hand to mouth and who deals with the

140

tooth, the whole tooth, and nothing but the tooth.

* Firemen: May this be the only way you are ever toasted.

* Press: To the freedom of the press and the success of its defenders. For it is the engine of our liberty, the terror of would be tyrants and the educator of the whole world.

* General: You can always tell a barber by the way he parts your hair.

You can always tell a dentist when you're in the dentist's chair.

Even an artist — you can tell him by his touch.

And you can always tell a_____(fill in appropriate profession).

But you cannot tell him much.

Some say there ain't no hell, but if they were never a_____

_____(fill in), how can they tell?

* Psychiatrists: He finds you cracked and leaves you broke.
                     He goes to a strip bar to study the audience.
                     His patients take their medicine lying down.

* Accountants: They really know the score in business because of all the deductions they make.

* Architects: Here's to the ivy that in time, covers their errors.

* Artists: They have to know when and where to draw the line.

* Banker: May he never lose his interest.

                     It's easy to get a loan — just prove you don't need it.

* Bosses: Here's to diapers and bosses — both are on your ass and usually full of crap.
                     Start worrying when he tells you not to worry.

* Builders: Even though each project starts in a hole, the work is often riveting.

*	Clergy:	By not drinking, you leave more for us.

*	Diplomats:	Who master the art of lying for their country while taking a lot, but saying nothing.

*	Doctors:	Who think that dressings have nothing to do with salads. May we always be your friend, but never your patient.

*	Education:	To the principal who does well even when he loses his faculties.

*	Lawyers:	Good lawyers know the law well. Great lawyers know the judge well.

To lawyers —	You may be able to live without them, but you certainly can't die without them. The best legal advice I ever received: Say it with flowers. Say it with eats. Say it with kisses. Say it with sweets. Say it with jewelry. Say it with drink.

But always be certain
Never to say it with ink.

*   Army:

To the soldier who fights and loves. May he always be the winner in both of these encounters.

*   Navy:

Here's to the ships of our Navy
And to the ladies of our land.
May the first be well rigged
And the latter well manned.

*   Marines:

If ever you look on heaven's scenes,
The streets will be guarded by
The United States Marines.

*   Military:

Here's to our military
And the battles they have won.
Here's to America's hues,
The colors that never run.

*   Politicians:

To an honest politician who, when he is bought, stays bought and stands for whatever the voters will fall for.

* Retirement: We don't know what we will do without you, but we sure are looking forward to finding out.

* Sales People: Here's to those who open doors and close deals.

* Speakers: The best speech is a short speech.

* Stockbrokers and Weather Forecasters:
    Who, most of the time, can tell you why something happened yesterday.

* Work: As Thoreau said, "If you do what you love, you will love what you do."

Miscellaneous Toasts

   * Do not resist growing old — many are denied that privilege.

   * Nothing about you is old — except for some of your jokes.

   * Now we know what separates the men from the boys — many years.

* To wine — it improves with age — the older I get, the more I like it.

* May you live as long as you want to, and want to as long as you live.

* Another candle on your cake?
  That's no cause to pout.
  Just be happy you have the strength
  To blow the damn thing out!

* Who'd want to be a bee and sip
  Sweet honey from the flowers lip
  When he might be a fly and steer
  Heads first into a glass of beer.

* Life would be really obscene
  Without a daily fix of caffeine.

* A glass in the hand is worth two on the shelf.

* Lift 'em high and drink 'em dry
  To the guy who says, "My turn to buy."

* One bottle for the (four) of us.
  Thank goodness there's no more of us.

* To your health. May we drink again in ten years time
And many more in-between.

* I drink to your health when I'm with you.
I drink to your health when I'm alone.
I drink to your health so often
I'm starting to worry about my own.

* Here's to our hosts, friendly and sweet
Your wit is endless, but when do we eat?

* Even though another year has passed
How come he's/she's no older than the last?

* May we all live in happiness and die free of debt.

* May we live to learn well
And learn to live well.

* May you live for two hundred years and be there to
blow out the candles.

* Here's to a guy (gal) who is never blue
Here's to a buddy who is always true
Here's to a pal no matter how big the load

He'll (she'll) never turn down
One more for the road.

* The more I drink, the better you sing.

* Too much work and no vacation
Deserves at least a small libation.
So cheer my friends and raise your glasses
Work's the curse of the drinking classes.

* I toast you with wine, whiskey and tonic
May the plagues you face be not bubonic.

* You may not have been the number one student, the top athlete or the homecoming queen, but we're proud of you anyway — son.

* Now that you have graduated, it's time to go out to become educated.

* We can't believe it's been_____years since you tied the knot.
If your marriage were a thermostat, it would say, "Hot, hot, hot!"

* Here's to you both

A happy pair
On the birthday of
Your love affair.

* Here's to the couple who have the wisdom to know it doesn't matter who wears the pants, as long as there's money in the pockets.

* Here's to your miracle — for you, it means you had a baby.
At my age, it means I won the lottery.

* To my boss — remember your job spelled backwards is double S O B.

* It's not that we think you worked here a long time, but when you started here, the Dead Sea only had a cold.

* I'm afraid we have some bad news — your entire 401K was invested in a company called "Soap on a Stick."

* To the good old days — we weren't that good because we weren't that old.

* May your new house be too small to hold all your friends.

* May your life be long and happy
Your cares and sorrows few
And the many friends around you
Prove fruitful, helpful and true.

* Here's wishing you the kind of troubles that will only last as long as your New Year's resolutions.

* Here's wishing you more happiness
Than all my words can tell
Not just alone for Christmas
But for the rest of the year as well.

* May every day of Hanukkah be a very happy one
And the spinning dreidel bring us lots of luck and fun.

* "Beauty is in the eye of the beerholder."

* "If you drink, don't drive — don't even putt."

* Here's to today and forget the past.
I hope you bought a car that will last.

*   Ashes to ashes

    Dust to dust

    Your new car is beautiful

    Just don't let it rust.

*   If at first you don't succeed — adjust your goals.

Relatives

*   Husbands/Fathers:

    Here's to Dad — if I could be but half the man he is, I will be very short. On the other hand, I will always look up to him no matter how tall I grow.

    May your life be long and sunny

    And your husband happy and funny.

    When a husband toasts a wife, all could be well.

    When a wife toasts a husband, all is well.

    Wives faults are many, husbands have only two: everything they say and everything they do.

*   Wives/Mothers:

    Here's to Eve — mother of our race

    Who wore a fig leaf in just the right place.

    And here's to Adam — father of us all

Who was Johnny on the spot

When the leaves began to fall.

Here's to some of the happiest hours of my life

Spent in the arms of another man's wife — my mother.

You can have a wife, you can have a lover,

But don't forget, your best friend is your mother.

A good wife (or husband) and health

Are a man's (or woman's) best wealth.

* Family:

To my family, who still seem to love me even though they know me best.

To my brothers or sisters, my uncles and aunts,

To the ones who wear dresses and the ones who wear pants.

I'm very happy that we've gathered here.

But even more glad that it's just once a year.

* Son:

We gave you life

We gave you clothes

We gave you milk and honey.

Now that you're on your own

Mom and I spend all the money.

*   Daughter:

We've seen you grow from a little girl

Into a woman of style.

We'd tell you this even more often

If you'd come home once in awhile.

*   Grandparents:

Let us raise our glasses

Then let us imbibe

To the wonderful couple

Who started this tribe.

*   Brother:

Remember — you're just an "R" away from being a bother.

*   Sister:

To my sister

You listen to my woes

But when you're not looking

I wear all your clothes.

*   Other:

153

To my aunts, uncles and cousins — I love you all, but remember that to me, everything is relative.

Sports

*   Baseball:

To our MVP — May you never be caught off base while playing the field.

*   Coaches:

To our coach — For whom sweat is sweeter than wine.

*   Fishing:

May good things come to those who bait.

A bad day at fishing is better than a good day at work.

Here's to our fisherman brave
Here's to those fish he caught.
Here's to those who got away
And here's to those he bought.

*   Golf:

Here's to Jim who continues to miss holes-in-one by just 6 to 8 strokes.

Here's to your woods, here's to your irons, here's to your putter too. May the balls you hit with them drop in the hole for you.

* Sailing:

May your sails never fail — Down the hatch!

* Tennis:

To tennis — where you always get served, but love means nothing.

* Camping:

Life as a camper is just one canned thing after another.

* Fishing:

Here's to the fish that I may catch
So big that even I
When bragging of it afterwards
Will never have to lie.

* Team:

Losing the big game is worse than death. At least with death, you don't have to face the next day.

I know with this crowd of true sportsmen — it's not whether you win or lose that counts, as long as you beat the point spread.

Let us remember, "The race is not always to the swift nor the battle to the strong — but that's the way to bet."

The only failure is not trying your best.

* Hockey:

That's the thing they play between fights.

* Shooting:

It's hard to find a person of your caliber.

* Football:

Passing, kicking, illegal use of hands

That's not on the field

That's just in the stands.

* Waterpolo:

To all the horses who have drowned playing this game.

Weddings — The Most Traditional Toast Occasion:

* May you be poor in misfortune

Rich in blessings

Slow to make enemies

And quick to make friends.

* As you slide down the banister of life,

May the splinters never point the wrong way.

* May your troubles be less

And your blessings be more

And nothing but happiness

Come through your door.

* May your hearts be warm and happy

With the sound of joyous laughter

Every day and in every way

And forever and ever after.

* Here's to the bride and mother-in-law

Here's to the groom and father-in-law

Here's to sisters and brothers-in-law

Here's to friends and friends-in-law

May none of them ever need an attorney-at-law.

* Here's to the husband and here's to the wife

May they always be healthy and lovers for life.

* Here's to the bride

And here's to the groom

And here's to (Fill in appropriate name)

Who paid for this room.

* Down the hatch to a wonderful match.

* May all your ups and downs occur underneath your covers.

About the Author:

Larry Miller is a graduate of the City College of New York with a degree in electrical engineering. He has held a number of technical and managerial positions of increasing responsibilities. He retired in July 2000 after serving eleven years as the general manager of the Consumer Products Division of Seiko Instruments USA.

Throughout his career he has been called upon to give talks, make presentations and act as master of ceremonies at various events. This led to his developing a "specialty" in the area of roasts and toasts, which in turn has led to the writing of this book.

Printed in the United States
145146LV00003B/98/A